KIT COLEMAN
Queen of Hearts

Kit Coleman wrote about just about everything. From 1889 until her death in 1916, she held forth in the pages of the Toronto *Mail* on practically any subject imaginable—from advice to the lovelorn and tips on health and beauty, to reporting firsthand on the Spanish-American War in Cuba. Her personality, wit, and wisdom captivated readers throughout Canada. Here are the collected columns of North America's pioneer female journalist.

No topic fell outside the realm of Kit Coleman's "Woman's Kingdom." She had something to say about the Fabians—and about men's moustaches. About fashion—and women wrestlers. About vaudeville—and Canadian politics. About the feminists of her day—and the activities of the Anti-Corset League.

And no prominent personality escaped the barb of her pen. She inter-

(continued on back flap)

(continued from front flap)

viewed Sarah Bernhardt and William Randolph Hearst. She scooped an exclusive interview with the notorious swindler Cassie Chadwick and covered the sensational murder trial of Harry Thaw. She even traveled to London to report on Queen Victoria's Diamond Jubilee.

Funny, compassionate, at times outspoken and downright nasty, Kit Coleman was a first, and an original: a peppery redhead who wrote personality journalism . . . and who became a controversial personality in her own right. KIT COLEMAN collects the best of her writings to provide a fascinating social history of Canada and North America at the turn of the century.

TED FERGUSON

KIT COLEMAN

Queen of Hearts

1978

Doubleday Canada Limited, Toronto, Canada
Doubleday & Company, Inc., Garden City, New York

ISBN: 0-385-13447-9
Library of Congress Catalog Card Number 77-92211
Copyright © 1978 by Ted Ferguson
First Edition
Printed in the United States of America

To the memory of Frank McCool

"Why do men look ashamed if they are caught reading the woman's page in a newspaper? Are women utter idiots? Do men believe that there is not a word to be written for our sex beyond frills and fopperies?"

Kit Coleman, 1891

CONTENTS

CONTENTS

AUTHOR'S NOTE

Canadian journalism has changed in the last twenty-five years. The old-style reporter, flamboyant, underpaid, hustling day and night out of sheer love for his profession, is almost an extinct species. In his place we have a new breed—ultraconservative university graduates who show more concern for their pension plans and mortgage payments than they do for their daily assignments.

The introduction of higher wages and shorter hours by the American Newspaper Guild after World War Two is largely responsible for this, the quietest of revolutions. Journalism has become a more respectable profession, attracting more respectable people; the ex-gamblers, ex-priests, ex-drifters who used to abound in our newsrooms are no longer wanted. On some metropolitan newspapers even the copy boys have attended university. To give them credit, the new breed has improved the over-all quality of the writing: news stories are more compact, more grammatically correct, and the coverage of labor, finance, and other specialized sectors has a much more knowledgeable ring to it.

But I cannot help thinking that something valuable has been discarded. Canadian newspapers are duller today; they sorely need the colorful characters whose personal vitality so often enlivened the stories they wrote.

When I first entered journalism in the early 1950s, there were still a few old-timers around. I have memories of Barney crawling through a hotel air shaft to listen in on a closed govern-

mental meeting; of Gerry producing fascinating crime reports
when not sleeping on his desk (he did not like wasting money on
paying rent); of Colin coming to a newsroom party with seven
chorus girls, a carload of oysters, and beer he had conned out of
a Mafia nightclub owner; of Barry, a rabbi's son, wearing a Nazi
arm-band to gate-crash a neo-fascist gathering.

Hardly any journalists show an inclination for that sort of behavior nowadays. And if they do, they are quickly discouraged.
Not only by strict union-management regulations, but by the
sterile atmosphere of the newsrooms themselves. Newsrooms
used to be noisy, paper-strewn places where local misfits
dropped in to talk, play poker, or share a bottle. With their gray
metal desks, potted plants, carefully arranged bulletin boards,
and front-door guards (to keep the misfits out), most modern
editorial offices generate as much fun as the average insurance
company. (At a Montreal paper where I worked in the mid-
1960s, the reporters were cautioned against raising their voices
unless a major story was breaking. Consequently, we all tiptoed
around, reverently, as though it were Notre Dame Cathedral.)

Which brings me to Kit Coleman. I first heard of her in 1976
when I noticed her column in the *Toronto Mail* while I was
doing research for a TV documentary at the University of Alberta's microfilm section. Her bright comments intrigued me so
much that I went through two years of microfilm, just reading
Kit. Before I left the university that day, I realized she was the
kind of journalist we seem so foolishly bent on eliminating—a
distinct character and a courageous, hard-working writer.

I also knew that her contribution to Canadian letters should
not stay buried in microfilm vaults. Encouraged by Doubleday
editors Betty Jane Corson and Rick Archbold, I spent the better
part of a year researching Kit's personal life and selecting items
from "Woman's Kingdom." This book does not pretend to be a serious, in-depth study of the 1890s and early 1900s. Instead, it is
meant to entertain the reader, as Kit's column did when she was
writing it.

                                                    Ted Ferguson

INTRODUCTION

The phenomenon of the New Woman had a stunning impact when it burst upon the North American scene in the late 1800s. Young ladies began rejecting Victorian concepts of genteel femininity and proper public behavior: they smoked cigarettes, rode bicycles, abandoned chaperons, talked politics, played golf and tennis, and, perhaps the biggest shock of all, demanded jobs in male-dominated professions.

These pioneering feminists were, naturally enough, mocked, scorned, or thoroughly detested by almost every man in Canada. Women, they felt, should restrict their activities to the kitchen, the marriage bed, and the nursery; there was no finer pursuit for a woman than to demurely serve her husband and children. Yet there were some males who realized there could be advantages to be gained in letting more females invade the professions. Christopher Bunting was one of them. As managing editor of the *Toronto Mail,* he wanted to fatten the newspaper's circulation so that he would not have to depend so heavily on printing railway tickets to keep it solvent. Bunting figured that if women were actually reading newspapers—something they supposedly rarely did in the past—they might be inclined to buy the *Mail* if it carried a special women's page every Saturday.

What he had in mind was a harmless hodgepodge of recipes, fashion reports, and hints on etiquette. Even the staunchest feminist, he reasoned, must be interested in those things. The woman he hired in 1889 to write the page had an entirely different idea in mind. Within a few months of launching her "Woman's Kingdom" column, Kathleen "Kit" Coleman, a peppery, indefatigable redhead, was turning out some of the most inventive, most discussed pieces of journalism ever published in Canada. The recipes were there, and so were the fashion notes and the finger-bowl tips, but they were lost in a flurry of items commenting on the arts, politics, contemporary personalities, social mores, and—to the utter disgust of many Victorians who believed such a topic did not belong in a newspaper—romance.

Kit was Canada's first advice-to-the-lovelorn columnist. Her advice to troubled readers often mirrored the hard-gained wisdom of the worldly lady who, before she was twenty-six, had gone through two husbands and was forever declaring in print that she did not want a third. (To an affection-hunting wife, for instance, she wrote, "How can your husband sanely attend to his business if you are always hanging on his shoulder when he comes home, tearful and red-nosed, telling him he doesn't love you anymore? You are so stupid. Imagine tearing up a plant every few days to look at the roots to see if it is growing!")

But Kit was more than just a desk-bound columnist. She was a globe-traveling reporter who covered the Spanish-American War —and, in doing so, becoming the first accredited woman war correspondent in history—the Chicago World Columbian Exposition, Queen Victoria's Diamond Jubilee celebration, and the sensational Harry Thaw murder trial. She also interviewed the likes of William Randolph Hearst, Sarah Bernhardt, Eleonora Duse, and Lillie Langtry; and she scooped the entire North American press corps when she got into a Cleveland jail cell to talk to the notorious swindler Cassie Chadwick.

The lengths to which Kit would go to get a story amazed her less-dedicated colleagues. So did her almost total disregard for her own appearance. Kit bustled about the corridors of power— in Ottawa, Washington, and London—wearing the same frumpy dresses or wrinkled blouses she wore in the newspaper composing room: she seldom noticed the ink stains on her hands and clothing, and she kept her naturally curly hair in a casual upsweep because it was easier to manage that way. Her drab, unfashionable looks made her appear at least ten years older than she really was. When she was nearing forty, a reader wrote to say that she and her husband had seen Kit at a horse show, and they were appalled:

"Here is what we saw: a tall, gaunt, passé woman, nearer to fifty than forty, gowned shabbily in an old black silk that smelled of ammonia (we passed close to you, Madam), and wearing a hat—a dusty, old chip hat, laden with ancient feathers, which matched your air of shabby gentility; old black kid gloves, printers'-inked at the fingertips, and large feet, encased in merely passable shoes; a face like a mask, powdered heavily, impassive, hard, cruel. That's what you looked like, Madam. Yet here you are with your 'clever' criticisms of people whose shoes you would not be permitted to blacken."

No doubt Kit was a disturbing sight, but the "impassive, hard, cruel" face the reader saw was not an accurate reflection of her true personality. Kit was a warm and sympathetic lady, well liked by some of her co-workers and absolutely adored by the others. She was, however, given to sporadic temper eruptions. One such blowup occurred when an elegantly dressed, full-bearded gentleman stormed into the newspaper office to protest against something Kit had written. Spotting her sitting at a desk, clipping items from a paper, the man accused Kit of being irresponsible and immoral. Kit jumped up and, working the scissors furiously, pretended she was going to cut off his beard. The man fled, but the next day he had a messenger deliver a note to her, demanding an apology. "I sincerely regret that you feared I was attempting to de-beard you," Kit said in her reply. "I can understand what an affront to your dignity it must have been to have an irrational, angry woman threaten such a beautiful growth. I assure you, sir, that I had no intention of harming your beard. I was aiming for your nose, which I felt required trimming, as it was so large it could not help poking into other people's affairs."

Despite her temper and her dowdy appearance, men were drawn to Kit. Even rigid traditionalists, opposed to the slightest alteration in womankind's status, found themselves charmed by her intelligence, wit, confident manner, and, it was said, the loveliest sherry-brown eyes in all the Dominion. Kit received no less than five marriage proposals after her second husband died. She spurned them all until, at thirty-four, she surrendered to a persistent campaign waged by an Ontario physician, Dr. Theobald Coleman. Their union was not blissfully happy (he did not like charging working-class patients for his services and, alas, he was a poor breadwinner). But Kit was more contented with the soft-spoken, kindly doctor than she had been with her previous mates, both of whom were arrogant, domineering and cold.

Kit's first husband, George Willis, had been a wealthy country squire forty years her senior. Born Kathleen Blake near Galway in western Ireland, she was sixteen when her parents arranged to have her marry Willis. Kit belonged to an old, established family (her uncle was the noted Dublin orator Rev. Tom Burke) that had plenty of prestige but a dwindling supply of money. A landowner and antique dealer, her father rode to the hounds, had Irish writers and artists for dinner guests, and, a social-minded idealist, helped organize movements to feed and clothe widows, orphans, and other underprivileged people. He passed on many of his liberal attitudes to Kit and, by matching her up with Willis, he hoped to take care of her future monetary needs too.

Willis sent his young bride to blue-ribbon schools in Dublin and Brussels but, apart from gratitude for allowing her to acquire a better education than she would in rural Ireland, she had no feeling whatsoever for him. As for his motive for marrying Kit, he wanted to prove his virility, but apparently Kit did not engender enough proof, for he was constantly chasing other women. When Kit was twenty, Willis died, leaving his fortune to the one woman he really loved, his aged mother. Kit sold some of the Willis mansion furniture and went to England, planning to get a fresh start by emigrating to Australia or South Africa. The first boat out of Liverpool was going to Canada, and, too impatient to wait around, she bought a passage on it. Arriving in Toronto in 1884, Kit supported herself doing secretarial work until she married her boss, Edward Watkins. The couple moved to Winnipeg and had two children. (Kit mentioned the children often in her column, saying what a handsome boy Thady was or how Pat lost her doll at the park. Both practically idolized their mother but she stopped writing about them when they reached adolescence and said her remarks were making them targets of schoolyard teasing. Thady grew up to work in a bank and to join the Toronto Argonaut Rowing Club; Pat married an affluent farmer.)

Watkins' sudden death in 1889 from a heart attack left Kit a widow again and, as both marriages had been stifling affairs, she returned to Toronto intent on establishing a permanent career.

Journalism was an ideal choice. Since childhood Kit had wanted to be a writer. Her literary heroes were Dickens and

Shakespeare and, knowing she did not have the genius to produce great works, she decided to try and earn her living writing articles. She had no writing experience, except for a few unpublished poems and short stories, but that did not deter her from submitting articles to Canadian magazines. E. E. Shepherd, the publisher of *Saturday Night*, bought one of her articles, an essay on the Bohemians she had observed in Paris during a long-ago summer holiday. Upon reading it in the magazine, Christopher Bunting hired the twenty-five-year-old widow as Canada's first full-time women's page editor.

The half-dozen women working in Canadian editorial rooms were thought to be disreputable specimens of warped femininity. Prostitutes and saloon dancers rated lower on the social scale but, in some people's minds, not all that much lower. Because their editors had little respect for them, female reporters were handed the worst assignments: obits, high-society functions, whatever else the male reporters preferred not to do. If a woman got a job on a newspaper, it was usually due to her willingness to accept a smaller wage than a male journalist. The prospect of having to fight a herculean battle—to prove that women could do as well as men and should be respected for their professionalism—appealed to Kit almost as strongly as the idea of making her living with a pen.

Kit's initial columns covered half a page and bore the short-lived heading "Fashion Notes and Fancies for the Fair Sex." That half page soon blossomed into a whole seven-column page, and when Kit was in a particularly expansive mood that called for more space, the editors obligingly carried the tail end of "Woman's Kingdom" over into another part of the paper.

Her early writing included a provocative sketch in which a husband scolds his wife for not reading a newspaper. The wife boldly returns the sally, saying she would read the paper if there was something interesting to women in it. Bunting did not like that essay, nor did he like the caustic remarks on selfish husbands, inept politicians, and the lack of ethics among Canadian businessmen that crept into the column. However, he told Kit to continue writing as she pleased. At least until he assessed the public response. As it happened, the public either loved "Woman's Kingdom" or was shocked by it, but Bunting was delighted because, no matter how people reacted, they bought the paper to read it.

"Woman's Kingdom" ran for twenty-one years. It did not offset the paper's nagging debt, and the *Mail* was forced to merge with the more successful *Empire* in 1895. The new paper was henceforth known as the *Mail and Empire*.

After leaving Winnipeg, Kit and her two children had moved into a shabby Toronto boardinghouse that catered to university students. While Thady and Pat were at school, Kit sat at a rolltop desk writing. She wore a man's black velvet smoking jacket and, because she was near-sighted, held the pens and pencils she used an inch from her nose. Her pet white rat, Patsy Brannigan, darted about the untidy, austere room. Once a week Kit would ride the streetcar to the newspaper office to read the mail and to supervise the setting up of her page. If the printers grumbled about her awful handwriting, she would bring in her column the following week in a twenty-foot strip, the pages pasted together, just to really get their dander up.

Kit was a bit of a tyrant when it came to smoking and drinking. It was all right for men to do both—in moderation—but if a woman dared light up or became inebriated in her presence, she was likely to scold her vigorously. Kit was in a posh Ottawa restaurant when the middle-aged wife of a prominent civil servant, sitting alone at a nearby table, lit a prelunch cigarette. Kit asked her to put it out and the woman, visibly annoyed, complied. After her meal the mandarin's wife took another cigarette from her purse and, tossing Kit a defiant glance, proceeded to smoke it. Kit summoned the waiter and urged him to remove the woman to the alley. When the puzzled waiter asked why, Kit replied, "Because that is where the rest of the trash is kept."

Kit's husband, Theobald, was among the select few who could enter the Coleman home three sheets to the wind and not be chastised. Her friend Jean Blewett recalled visiting Kit on a winter night when the good doctor came home drunk. "He's a very cautious man," Kit said, excusing him. "He's been consuming alcohol to ward off a bad cold. Before the cold appears."

Although she chose to overlook whatever drinking her husband did, Kit was a temperance crusader. She opposed all-out prohibition, and she thought pipe smoking was a charming male pastime, but she felt certain that excessive smoking and drinking, by either sex, would result in moral ruination. Her attitudes were actually considered too tolerant by some members of the ladies' temperance organizations that had taken root across Canada. They advocated banning the devil weed and the demon brew altogether, and they were not too keen on sex either. Going into the twentieth century, Canadian temperance leaders were still publicly promoting the Victorian idea that if you had sexual intercourse more than once a month with your husband you'd risk giving birth to physically deformed babies.

Kit liked to say that nothing on earth surprised her. Especially not the actions of women in love or the private conduct of men who passed themselves off in public as pillars of virtue. But she admitted to being amazed, and somewhat baffled, by a press colleague's disclosure that Sir Wilfrid Laurier read her column faithfully. She could not envision the Prime Minister, whom she felt was a brilliant though sometimes politically misguided soul, pushing vital governmental documents aside to make room on his desk for "Woman's Kingdom." Intensely curious, she asked an Ottawa reporter to find out why Laurier liked her column.

Since the reporter never completed his mission, it remained for Kit herself to question the Prime Minister. Spotting him at an Ottawa garden party, Kit approached Laurier and, after a brief conversation, inquired as to his favorite "Woman's Kingdom" feature, the love letters, the celebrity interviews, or what? The P.M. said there was no one feature he preferred; he read the column because he could never guess what she would be writing about next. His answer must have pleased Kit for some readers actually complained that she had too much variety in her writing. A Hamilton man wrote to Bunting requesting that Kit be replaced by a male journalist as "the manner in which she grasshoppers [sic] from subject to subject on a single page proves women do not have the power of concentration necessary to accomplishing a first-rate job." A Toronto teacher sent Kit a letter saying he would not allow his sixteen-year-old daughter even to look at the "Woman's Kingdom" page. "You change topics so frequently that one cannot tell whether portions of your column will be suitable for the eyes of an innocent child or will be utterly shocking."

Kit's brash, unladylike statements, and particularly her attacks on the behavoral pattern of the male animal, thrust her into the forefront of the New Woman movement. She did not relish being there. Women should strive for equality in the professions, she said, but they should not do so in their private lives.

"The New Woman movement is a fine one in moderation," she wrote. "But it overshoots its mark when it makes a vain effort to equalize the sexes, the chief charm of which is that they can never be equalized. They are each the beautiful component of the other. Until nature changes her laws and God alters His creation, it will always be thus. Two unequal sexes fitting wonderfully together."

Marriage was the greatest career a woman could aspire to, but, she said, if a woman had as much ill fortune as she herself did in trying to secure a worthy mate, she must be encouraged to carve out a place in the workaday world. And, Kit warned, those stuffy, obstinate males blocking womankind's progress had better step aside, lest they be rudely shoved. "The man who stands in the path of the New Woman can be compared to an idiot attempting to force back a tidal wave with a cricket bat."

In 1898, Kit finally married her relentless suitor, Dr. Coleman. The following year he was appointed company doctor at Copper Cliff, a northern Ontario mining community, and Kit reluctantly consented to live in that isolated town. The Colemans arrived during a smallpox outbreak and Kit filled in as an emergency nurse, all the while writing "Woman's Kingdom" and sending it to Toronto via horseback and train.

Understandably, she loathed Copper Cliff. The landscape was barren from the effects of sulphur smoke, and the cultural scene was just as bleak. Kit wrote about Copper Cliff in such negative terms—referring to the community as a Canadian Siberia—that the townsfolk were overjoyed when Dr. Coleman resigned his post. The couple settled in Hamilton, Ontario, in 1901. Dr. Coleman opened a private practice and Kit plunged into two new hobbies, raising prize-winning Bedlington terriers (she won every award for the breed at the 1903 American Bench Show in New York) and riding her horse over Hamilton Mountain and along the Dundas Marsh.

Her domestic life did not interfere with her newspaper travels.

Whenever a story idea intrigued her, she approached Bunting for expense money, which he usually provided the same day. He never tried to curb her traveling, even though she charged the paper for side trips (to Tijuana after the Hearst interview for instance), because she turned in a good article wherever she went. But he did restrict her to a skimpy expense account, a fact she often mentioned in her column.

Bunting raised Kit's salary in the early 1890s to $35 a week, the same wage paid the star male reporters. Yet, oddly enough, when Kit sought a small raise in 1911 for a front-page column she was ordered to write in addition to "Woman's Kingdom," the new managing editor said no. Enraged, Kit quit her job and began selling "Woman's Kingdom," without the lovelorn segment and renamed "Kit's Column," to dozens of dailies and weeklies across Canada. She thus became the nation's first syndicated columnist. Kit charged $5.00 a column and earned more than she had as a staff writer. With a touch of malice, she would not let her old newspaper run the column, regardless of the fee it offered her.

Free-lancing had one major disadvantage. If she was ill, Kit had to produce a column anyway or lose her income. So she turned out many a column while lying in bed, drinking tea and scribbling on notepaper. In May 1915, Kit went to bed with a terrible cold, expecting to write her column as usual. The cold developed into pneumonia, which, at the age of fifty-one, ended her life. By that time Kit had long since won the respect she had fought for in her profession and, in gaining it, had influenced many editors to change their minds about assigning women reporters better jobs. In her path followed such journalistic trailblazers as Faith Fenton, who covered the Klondike Gold Rush for the *Toronto Globe;* Cora Hind, who was named the first female agricultural editor in Canada by the *Winnipeg Free Press* in 1909; and *Toronto Globe* columnist Jean Blewett. The last, in fact, was a leading poet signed on by the *Globe* to compete with Kit, but it was no contest. Blewett lacked Kit's humor, punch, and sheer show-business pizzaz, and if the *Globe* editors hoped for a weekly circulation-building catfight between the two, they were disappointed. Kit and the poet became fast friends and were forever tossing bouquets to each other in print. It was Blewett who crowned Kit "the Queen of Hearts." In a *Globe* piece she wrote that Kit "not only writes of the affairs of the heart when she renders romantic advice, but she touches our hearts with everything she does. Whether in laughter, or sadness, or anger. She is the Queen of Hearts, the supreme monarch of all of our emotions."

Most of the material in this book is from the 1890s, when Queen Victoria was on her throne—and Queen Kit on hers.

1. CITY LIGHTS

Toronto was fairly bursting with civic pride over its new city hall. Eight years in construction, the red sandstone structure was a showplace of mahogany and marble and, taking heed of the smallest of details, doorknobs bearing the city's coat of arms. Mayor John Shaw and his council rode to the ribbon-cutting ceremony in September 1899 in two streetcars, each pulled by twelve gray horses. In the weeks that followed, thousands of Torontonians flocked to the Bay and Queen Street locale to tour the $2.5 million building. Despite a strong streak of civic conceit, Kit was not as ecstatic about the city hall as she was about the sparsely furnished sanctuary that opened its doors five years later on Yonge Street. Kit and twelve other lady writers had banded together to found the Canadian Women's Press Club and, having more zeal than money, they had to settle in a third-story garret. Appointed the club's first president, Kit stated in a 1904 report, "This is the realization of a long, long dream for me. Our city hall is a beautiful spot but it is merely an office building. Our club is a home." Kit donated a carpet to the club, bought flowers to fill vases, and arranged fund-raising social events. A chic ladies' club housed on the second floor wanted Kit for a member but she preferred the cozy, far less opulent garret. Besides the steadily growing ranks of women reporters, the CWPC became a meeting place for VIPs passing through town and artists from nearby studios. Kit was the club's most sought-after conversationalist. Katherine Hale said in a 1956 book, Toronto: The Romance of a Great City, *that Kit "represented all that every journalist longed to be." Moreover, Hale said, the garret atmosphere "suited her kind of bohemianism—an appreciation of the out-of-the-way and a camaraderie that was at once sincere and unpretentious." Relaxing at the club, Kit heard local anec-*

*dotes and deplorable-situation tales that she personally checked
out before turning them into column items. She was, in fact, a
tireless chronicler of Toronto life, and many of her stories re-
flected the concerns of the average citizen.*

Our poor Mayor is daily besieged by lovely women—that large
and serious force of workers who demand "just a bare room" in
the civic building wherein to prosecute their reforms on the
world. The National Council of Women is too deserving and too
powerful an organization to be lightly set aside. The request is a
modest one of an unfurnished room. They ought to have it.

"I haven't weakened a bit," is the reply of His Worship. Do
"weaken" Mr. Mayor. You know perfectly well that it is on the
backs of women the world is carried. We may not be able to
vote, sir, but we control a lot of votes; we do a lot of work
behind the scenes, and more of the marionettes who dance before the public are set in motion by the hands of women than
you, perhaps, Mr. Mayor, are aware of. If the hand that rocks
the cradle rules the world, then men in public positions had better be good to that little hand. Give the women a room, sir, and
consider the Mayor's chair yours, rent free, for the rest of your
life.

Married couples living in what are known as family hotels in
Toronto rarely speak during meal-times. Husbands and wives
will sit down and rise in absolute silence. When a third party
stops for a moment's parley, the couple brighten up and indulge
in persiflage on the state of the weather or the breakdown of the
hotel elevator. Then, left by themselves, they are stricken dumb
again. Why? Is there nothing left for discussions?

A great many letters have reached me lately regarding the pathetic figure who stands daily at the corner of Richmond and
Temperance Streets, offering the book on his life and other odds
and ends for sale. I allude to Captain W.D. Andrews, the famous
life-saver. The man is stone blind, having lost his sight through
an injury to the optic nerve caused mainly by exposure. He
wears a shabby coat covered with the medals presented by hu-

mane societies and royalties in recognition of a brave man's service to humanity.

We always reward so generously with decorations and medals. They cost so little and are easy to give. After decorating a hero thus, we let him beg in the streets. Captain Andrews has received the thanks of many parents whose children he saved from drowning. He stands on a Toronto street corner, shabby, blind, a living monument to the gratitude of humanity. People drift by without seeing him. Out of the people he has saved is there not one who will remove this blind hero from the streets and see that he is sufficiently cared for somewhere? It would seem there is not.

Stabbing is not a British habit. The knife is incurably distasteful to the colonials of British ancestry, as well as to Englishmen. The weapons of your Britisher are his fists; of the American, the revolver; the stiletto or dagger are the modes of the Italian and the Spaniard. There is something despicable about murder by the dagger. It is the most cowardly of all the weapons, and the man behind it is lower on the criminal scale than the thug or sandbagger.

I once saw a man who had eight knife wounds inflicted by quarelling Italians. Fortunately, not one of them was fatal. He was sincerely intoxicated when he was wounded, which perhaps accounts for his immunity from stabs to a vital spot. There is some spirit which guides the wandering footsteps of Alcohol's votaries and protects them from fatalities which often over-take the sober.

Poor Hoban and Marlowe, inoffensive English-speaking men, who were trying to stop a quarrel—evidently a foolish thing to do when the contestants are foreigners—paid the penalty of what might be called their Good Samaritanism. It is hoped that the authorities will get sharply after the criminals, and it must also be remembered that we have no better or more law-abiding citizens than many families of Toronto's Italian colony. The knife, however, seems to be the national weapon of Italy and Sicily, which may well do in those countries but should be effectively put down in this.

Camp-stool etiquette upon the Toronto ferry-boats is rather com-
plicated; largely, perhaps, because no one has yet taken the
pains to define it. In the first place, there aren't anything like
enough camp-stools to go around, save on very slimly-attended
trips, and, in the second place, every passenger upon whatever
kind of trip would like to appropriate two stools—one to sit
upon, the other to rest her (or his) feet upon. Not only etiquette
but mathematics is involved in the situation where there are
twice as many passengers as there are camp-stools.

As a rule, the man without a camp-stool threads his way along
the crowded deck until he spots a passenger who looks extra
soft-hearted and then he lays his hand upon her foot-stool and,
with a pleading look, asks if he may have it. Of course, the soft-
hearted passenger lets him have it. She has rushed to get on the
ferry and to pre-empt her two stools, and the man has taken his
time and poked about the boat; but she is the victim. Procras-
tination is not only the thief of time, but evidently of camp-stools
too.

The truth is, ferry-boats ought to provide more stools. Two
to a passenger is, after all, a meagre calculation. Some of the
ferry-boat commuting women bring out from town bundles
enough to load twenty stools, and they prefer to occupy stools
where they, and the bundles, may be cool and comfortable, and
enjoy the breezes and the view. The sooner a definite etiquette
concerning the whole matter is decided upon, the better for all—
especially for her who looks soft-hearted.

A well-known Toronto judge has a strange habit, while sitting in
court, of sucking one end of a quill pen, while the other end rests
in a large black ink-bottle on the bench in front of him. His
Lordship's ink-bottle is filled with brandy.

Why have we not shilling cabs in Toronto? Many a time one
would hire a hansom and go across town in it, rather than shiver
for twenty minutes waiting for a street car which, when it arrives, has no seat to offer you. Why is it that in Montreal and
Quebec one can enjoy the privacy of a cab ride for a comparatively small sum while, if you take one of the frowsy, unclean ve-
hicles that line up outside Union Station, you are compelled to

pay seventy-five cents to be jolted four blocks. The horses, too, that draw these shabby caravans are lean beasts, towards whom some human charity should be directed. Surely, in a city that is positively the most brilliant in the Dominion some change for the better might be afforded in the matter of transportation.

Did you ever get the cut from a fashionable acquaintance because you were carrying a parcel? I got a present of a piece of cloth and, not being able to get a messenger from the store, I went with a parcel nearly as long as myself, wrapped up in whitey-blue paper. I suppose it is not the correct thing in Canada, marching up a promenade such as King Street at four in the afternoon with a parcel four feet long. I daresay it is not "correct" to carry even a pair of gloves up King Street unless they are on your hands. I met a very fashionable dame. She stared at me, then the parcel—at me again—and fled up the street. She lost a rubber as she flew, and never waited to pick it up. I never saw anyone look so scared.

Why do women not get their shoes cleaned from dirt when out on a sloppy day far from home? It wouldn't be a bad idea to start girl bootblacks for ladies. There are countless girls who would be glad to earn five cents in this way. If women object to having their shoes blacked on the street, why does not an enterprising person start bootblack shops staffed by girls? I have never hesitated to have my shoes shone by a Johnny whenever I wanted it, but one would prefer a quiet place for this purpose, where a crowd would not gather and poke fun at one's number sevens.

Coroner Greig's jury returned a verdict of accidental death in the case of Willie Curran, who was killed by a street car in this city. Was it in a spirit of irony that these twelve good men added the rider that "a better fender might have saved the little one's life"? How long will the residents of this city permit themselves to play doormat to the self-seeking representatives who are supposed to govern municipal affairs? At least three perfect fenders have been submitted to the Mayor. Nothing has been done, and probably nothing will be done until the child of some wealthy, influential citizen is killed by the present fender in use. That fender is an open trap for any young children who have fallen to the ground. Why, the wonder of it is that the mothers of Toronto do not rise in a body and protest against inhumane carelessness that permits this wanton sacrifice of child-life. We are ready enough to proclaim against cruelty to animals, but we ignore the criminal carelessness that allows a corporation to play fast and long with human life.

Husbands ought to be made to live out during spring-cleaning time. All they do is grumble, as if that were any help, and as if they were the big sufferers. Special house-cleaning clubs should be opened for the accommodation of married men. We don't want them around, falling over pails and sliding down soapy passages, and growling if there isn't a lovely dinner ready with all the usual appointments.

It is earnestly hoped that the city fathers will not permit cemeteries to encroach on the town. The dead ought to be kept as far apart from the living as possible. We all know we have to die. Daily—nay, hourly—the hearses stalk the streets. We do not need the sight of gaunt monuments to remind us. Can't Toronto do as other cities have done and set apart beautiful parks for the dead? Must they be thrust under the very paving stones of our city? The matter is serious. Some people may prefer the dead to their present neighbors, but, I'm certain, they are in the minority.

A temperance orator was holding forth on the horrors of drink, and closed his lurid oration by asking, "What can be worse than the sight of a tender child guiding its drunken mother home through the rain at night?" A funny man had a ready answer. "Why," he exclaimed, "to see a tender mother leading home her drunken child!"

I often read with wonder of the fines and imprisonments that are inflicted upon persons arraigned under the plea of attempted suicide. Every human being has a right to hang, drown or poison himself if he wants to. The law allows a man to lose his soul by being an atheist or a prize bigot; the law allows a man to poison himself slowly with tobacco or drink. But it will pop him in the jug if he tries on carbolic acid or takes an overdose of morphine. The law is as unreasonable as a jealous woman.

Have you ever watched women signalling street car conductors when they want to get off? It is usually with a stony stare, and a haughty toss of the head, or a wild, irritating jerk of a lifted forefinger, or a thrust forward of the whole hand with a look that seems to say that the owner just knows that the conductor is doing his best to take her past her street. Now and then a woman will jump up and down on her seat, like a hen on a hot griddle, and lean forward in a frantic endeavor to catch the conductor's eye, while poking the eye of her neighbor with her umbrella or parcel; or a lofty, languid young lady will intimate by a pose of her eyelids that she will permit the slave of the collection box to arrest progress of the vehicle. They have their troubles, have conductors.

They're all back again—the summer people. The girl who has done a lot of yachting and speaks as if she had been spending her time all year in cruising and is attired in a yacht costume night and day; the young man who played three games of golf and can't talk of anything but caddies and links; his friend who went in for tennis and is overwhelmingly anxious to convince you of the amount of muscle he has; the girl from the rich side who pronounces Charles as if it were two syllables; the man from the States who, hearing that the harsh American voice was objected to in Canada, has gotten his voice down so low you cannot hear a word he says and you are under the impression that he is suffering from a form of idiocy; the child who has been impertinent all summer and who has come back home in need of a systematic course of treatment from a professional spanker. They are all here again. The old joke is about to commence.

2. ADVICE OF THE HEART

Few journalists in Canada have ever had the following that Kit did. Men and women would go blocks out of their way to buy the Saturday Mail (and the Mail and Empire after the two papers merged) as it rolled off the presses in a four-story brownstone building at the corner of Bay and King streets. Society matrons, sweatshop girls, and businessmen were among her fans. Not surprisingly, the most eagerly read portion of "Woman's Kingdom" was the lovelorn column. Mail arrived at the newspaper office by the sackful and Kit labored late at night to sort through it. Wanting to conserve space so that she could answer more correspondents, she usually printed only her own replies, not the letters she received.

Kit referred to the letter writers as her "paper children," her "shadow children," and "dolls in need of mending." In her replies, she stressed the necessity for purity before marriage and truthfulness and fidelity once the knot was tied. The tone of Kit's remarks varied greatly: she could be humorous, maudlin, compassionate, and, at times, downright nasty. She sided with her feminine readers more than she did with the males, but women were assailed too: jealous wives, adultresses, and flirtatious virgins were her main targets.

Some correspondents displayed extraordinary tenacity in weathering Kit's attacks. A promiscuous housewife, signing her letters Hot-Blooded Cheat, wrote to "Woman's Kingdom" month after month, complaining of unhappy love affairs. Kit rapped her every time. Finally, despairing of all those sordid tales, Kit was compelled to write, "Your nauseating immorality and endless whining appal me. Please find someone else to listen to you. A priest, your mother, a deaf male, anyone but me." Three weeks later, Hot-Blooded Cheat was back with another sad story, and

Kit, forgetting her earlier outburst, consoled her by stating that she might be able to extinguish her wanton sexual fires by indulging in energetic bicycling sprees.

Maria: Asks me to tell her "what it signifies when a gentleman gets a lady's handkerchief and keeps it." It probably means, Maria, that he has a headcold.

Goose: The man who, after suggesting an improper course to you and being met with your indignation, writes "I have nothing to apologize for, I consider I took the proper method of finding you out," is a mean animal of the verminkind who needs the medicine of an honest man's horsewhip. His compliments as to your proved virtue are excessively sickening and his allusions to the fact that he tested his wife's purity before he married her places him outside the pale of decent society. Good little Goose —one of the first of my shadow children—I am so proud of you, so glad you gave that wretched cad his quietus. Oh, these brutes that attack our modest, young Canadian girls! How I wish I might go out with a shotgun and pot a score or two of the man-monkeys!

Lady Charlotte: I think the man must be a very poor specimen indeed. He engages you to marry him, then directly finds you have lost some of your money, so he jilts you. Then Fortune smiles on you a little and he comes whining back. How could you think of marrying such a flabby poltroon? I am afraid that you will not be very much better than him if you do. Perhaps this is for the best, as then you will be well-mated.

Ann: It was not pleasant for you to know that your private affairs were the topic of an afternoon tea gossip. Take heart, for your life, as you describe it, is so dull that the gossipers must have had a boring time.

Satan: You are full of faith, my dear devil, in spite of your satirical lines, and you are also head over heels in love, horns, hoofs and all. Write to her by all means but keep your atheistical tendencies and your pessimism out of the letter. Deal with the world humorously and lightly, Satan, and it will deal lightly by you.

Lionel: Your love story is a perfect pastoral. Ought you, a gentleman by birth and position, to marry a domestic servant and so offend your friends? I think not unless the girl works her way to your educational level. Could you not arrange to have her attend evening classes? She is only seventeen—quite a girl still. As matters now stand, I cannot advise you to marry her offhand. It would mean social ostracism for you.

Enas P.: Asks "Why should women have a different moral standard from that of men?" There are many good and timid people who think questions like this ought to be shirked. It is so polite, so genteel to shirk big, grim facts and to call them indelicate. But I will not play ostrich and bury my eyes and ears in sand. I do not believe there should be one moral code for man and another for woman. At the same time, because a man makes a beast of himself, there is no reason why a woman should do the same. Neither sex ought to indulge in loose living. Society women, you know, have the remedy in their hands. If they would ostracise all bad men, innocent girls would not be seduced, and the air would soon be purified.

Margaret Ellen: Very few girls wish to be thought dolls and nothing else. Even those girls who are nothing else but dolls have moments of conviction that to be pretty, to be brainless and useless, puts them at a disadvantage, except at picnics and parties. Dolls are terrors to mothers of boys. These poor ladies have a sad time of it when their boys pick on dolls to fly away from the home nest with. For the mothers know all about the sawdust packing inside. The boy doesn't. He sees only the painted face, the staring blue eyes, the golden hair. A mother's misery is never worse than when her boy lights on a doll. She would rather have him wedded to a healthy, quiet, well-bred young woman, of graceful but deliberate carriage; cheerful, educated, a devoted wife. I'm afraid you are a bit of a dolly, Margaret Ellen. That is why you don't get along with the woman you hope will be your mother-in-law. Suppose you try showing her you aren't quite such a doll as you look? Show her you can cook potatoes and grill a steak.

Patsy: My dear, it would not be right of the girl to so deceive the man she would marry. Believe me, she would be discovered when time took its toll of her, and she would run a keen chance of never being happy again. Granted that a woman, thirty-seven-years-old, looks ten years younger. That will not last. Women's looks go suddenly as when a child's finger knocks over a house of cards. Nature would step in and the tale would be told. Of course, if she is not directly asked how old she is, there is no need for her to tell, is there?

Mary Anderson: A wise woman, my good little Mary, until the magic gold circle is actually on her finger, keeps her real powers in the background.

Reuben, Reuben: I've been thinking what a silly chap you are. Toiling, spending, gambling, loafing around the corner bar. Stop it, old fellow. You are far too honest a man to let yourself go to the "deminition bow-wows." Remember your dead mother lying under the ground with her busy, patient hands folded—unable to raise them in any earthly way to help her boy now.

Green Lassie: Did I ever say there was such a thing as love after marriage? Dear me, how curious!

Merely A Woman: You are jealous of your husband's first love; jealous of his musings, his silence on occasion. That earlier love is a fact in his life that you cannot displace. Every human being coming to maturity whose mentality has been at all developed has a secret garden, a nook where lie the withered roses, the bitter-sweet remembrances of the past. Each human soul is absolutely alone. There is no absolute sharing or merging of the Ego. Respect the individuality of the man you love. His past does not belong to you. Let him walk in his garden. Take off those green spectacles, foolish woman, and see your husband with common-sense, clear eyes.

Amette: Wait and bide your time of asking. Men are never so charitable as after a good dinner.

Cranky: You say I always advise my paper children not to kiss men. Would you have me tell them to go ahead and do it! Says you: "If a young lady has a gentleman friend going off on a journey for a long time, why shouldn't she let him kiss her good-bye just as she would a young lady friend?" Why not, indeed? Only not just like a young lady friend. Allow for a slight difference. Alack, my days of kissing are over so I cannot comment too knowledgeably on that difference. Am I very shocking? No doubt, some prim body will be flapping about my ears for that in twenty-four pages of manuscript!

Anxious: Your case is by no means unusual. Women, especially if they are the hysterical type, frequently fall in love with their doctor. It is one of the amenities of the medical life.

Cricket: Poor Cricket! Poor, poor, little Cricket! I am so sorry for you. Still, I see plainly that you are climbing up the hillside to a broad top where the sweet winds blow, Cricket, and the outlook is broad and cheery, and there is such a breadth of blue sky and sunshine overhead! Take heart. It is a long climb, but you are getting there, even though you faint often by the wayside. Brave little woman, pulling the heavy burden up too! Would it make it easier for you to know that your letter heartened me and set me to pulling my cart up more briskly?

Bernadine: Drop the man, seeing he is indifferent. If only girls would refrain from forcing their attentions on men. Why send them presents when they are dumb? Why do the hunting? How often will I have to advise, in this column, women to have some dignity, to refrain from being the aggressor? Let the man do the hunting. There is not and never was nor will be a man whom I would deign to hunt after.

Roland: Opines that girls nowadays flirt more shamefully than their grandmothers did. How does he know? Did he ever flirt with one's grandmother?

Jim: You evidently have no affinity with the girl you have become acquainted with, and it is well the affair has gone no further. She may be, as you say, "a respectable, virtuous, meritorious, neat person, dutiful to her parents and helpful to others." But what avails all that if there is no magic fire, if neither of you feel the divine spark? The great question between the sexes is a question of affinity, and it is one of the things that differentiates man from other animals. If you are not much above the animal—and I have known many highly-respected persons who are not—any decent woman and any man, decent or not, will do. Then the couples might be selected by a judicious committee. Break away from her, young man. Break away.

Margaret: Girls are such fools to let young men take liberties with them, such as kissing and caressing. There are a limitless number of cads who are going for a "good time with the girls" and who are dishonorable men, without honest intentions of matrimony. Even if nothing impure occurs during this caressing, sickly sentimentality is very injurious to a girl. It ruins delicacy of feeling and soils one's ladyhood.

Gwendolin: Asks me to tell her how she can amuse a gentleman by small talk. Will I suggest something? With pleasure. Ask him what he thinks of this year's asparagus growth. Butter beans might follow—they are nice right now. You might drift to cold lamb or salad. Ask about the church choir boys, if they are well, and all that. If he likes cream on his strawberries is a fine topic. Perhaps he has done something—dug up Etruscan pottery or done the Pyramids. If so, read up in your Encyclo. Keep clear of Adam and Eve, and the emotions, and art. The bicycle is a safe subject. You might throw in an epigram. "Nothing that is worth knowing can be taught, it must be learnt." Or, "Dandyism is the assertion of the absolute modernity of caddishness." This will make him think you are clever, because he will not understand what you are driving at. Neither will you, but that doesn't matter.

Frances St. Hiliary: The man who yields up his will to the dupery of sexual fascination is rarely respected, even by the woman who dupes him. The soft infatuate comes to a bad end, weakening down from point to point until he falls into a condition of social and domestic imbecility. Even less happy is the infatuate who knowingly takes leave of his wits the moment he comes in sight of his dubious charmer, resuming them as soon as he is alone again, to rave against spells he can never resist, and the folly he will never overcome. You needn't be proud, Frances, because some miserable man is infatuated with you.

Pera: You aren't a marrying woman? Well, you may not be any the worse for that. A good many girls are now preparing to face a life of solitary blessedness.

W.E.M.: What nonsensical vanity! The town mouse looks with contempt on the country mouse, and will not accept happiness because the bumpkin, who could and would protect and care for the vain creature, is not, forsooth, quite as well-educated as herself. He is "high-principled, steady, good-tempered, affectionate," etc., but he mispronounces some words and, being an Englishman, drops an "h" now and then. And, horror of horrors, he leaves his teaspoon in his cup! By all means dismiss the man. For his sake, not yours. It would be cruel to allow him to marry a little cad.

Ottawa Tom: You are jealous, Master Tom. According to your story, you deserve to feel the pangs of the Green Monster. You have never proposed to her; you haven't the pluck to do so; and because she happened to be kind and pleasant to you, you have built up a superstructure of fancied masculine mastery and proprietorship. It will serve you right if the other man is a bit more courageous and wins her. I've not the slightest atom of patience with cowards who dwaddle round, and never pop the fatal question.

Betsy Trotwood: Did I ever feel the need for human sympathy? Why, Betsy Trotwood, of course I did, and often do now. Poor soul! asking me, in the name of God, not to be cruel! What a hard woman one must be! Why, little Betsy, I would be, I hope and pray, the last to cast a stone at some wounded human creature. Still, let us be logical, practical. The man is not worth the suffering. He is the kind of man who can't buy an apple from an old woman on a street corner without making her think that she is the only representative of her sex who has ever found favor in his sight. There are good men—and God bless them—loyal, valiant gentlemen, but there are also the queer sensuous male persons who play with a woman's vanity, with her hereditary sense of admiration, play with infinite cunning for, friend, they know our vain weaknesses and take advantage of them. Be wary, and reticent, and do not let yourself sink into a pit whence no one can lift you up.

J.H.: Do I believe in long engagements? Yes, for simple, pure, innocent girls and men. A pure young girl is the greatest factor towards good in a man's life, and while waiting for her, any decent young fellow would as soon pitch himself into a mire as do wrong. But for others—for young men and women in high society—engagements cannot be too short. Not that society people are immoral. Far be it for me to say so. But the atmosphere they exist in is false and sensuous, and there is time for familiarities. This idling and loafing about together, and familiarity, is an enemy to love.

Y.: "All your advice," you say, "will not stop the folly of girls." Perhaps not. But I shall offer it whenever the girl asks for it, and it may help some foolish virgins resist the blandishments of your noble sex.

3. MODERN TIMES

To the strict, genteel Victorian, the 1890s was the period when society seemed to go mad. The quick-lunch counter began replacing the gracious dining room; mass-advertising campaigns peppered billboards and storefronts with huge posters and vulgar slogans; young people were shunning tea and milk in favor of a dark, strange-tasting brew called Coca-Cola. None of these changes were as disturbing, though, as the bicycle boom. First introduced to Canada in the late 1880s, the new-fangled two-wheeler (equipped with pneumatic tires, a gear shift, and stop-on-a-dime brakes) crowded city streets. By 1892 there were 10,000 cyclists in Toronto; ten years later one out of every twelve Canadians owned a bike. Female cyclists challenged males to street races, old ladies protested that youths barreled along sidewalks knocking them down, and the parking problem was so severe that bikes lined building fronts, cluttered hallways, and made downtown alleys impassable. Canadian writer W. A. Robertson went so far as to predict, in his 1894 book Cycling, that the bike would end all marital conflict because ". . . everyone will feel so well and good-humored and disinclined to quarrel that no one will go to war."

The horse and carriage and the horse-drawn sleigh remained major winter conveyances but they were headed for extinction. Electric streetcars started rattling along Canadian streets in 1892 and Henry Ford's noisy, two-cylinder contraptions would doom the bicycle in 1904. Even rock-ribbed traditionalists must have liked some of the changes. The electric light, for instance, took over from coal-oil lamps and candles, while the telephone eliminated a lot of hustling around on minor errands. Kit had mixed thoughts about progress. She adored the short films shown in

penny arcades, she deplored the sudden proliferation of tele-
phones, and she lamented the demise of old-fashioned good
manners. Before the 1900s appeared, however, she had electricity
and a telephone in her home—and she was riding to the Mail
and Empire building astride a fancy two-wheeler bought at
Timothy Eaton's Yonge Street emporium.

The bicycle craze will be the cause of my death unless I take to
the wheel myself, which I have serious thoughts of doing. The
other night a bicycle ran into my ribs and damaged them. I appealed to an Island policeman (it was at Hanlan's) and he said
the only thing to do was to go home and nurse one's ribs and to
anathematize Adam for having had the superfluous one out of
which woman is constructed. All my enthusiasm for the wheel,
which I was fast getting to boiling pitch, suddenly grew cool at
this dig in the ribs.

Truly this promiscuous cycling of raw youths along the dark
sidewalks is a hidden danger, against which the city or the Island, or somebody, ought to provide for the safety of the community. Why not have more light? Or else prohibit wheeling on
the Island sidewalks? The track ought to be enough for wheelers,
or the roads over in the city. It is not a nice sensation to have the
silent steed butt into your side and inflict on that tender part of
your person a broad, black and blue patch.

Achille, Cleveland, Ohio: That was a frightful record you sent
me. Three people insane within one day from over-work! Where
is the remedy in these days of hurry? I assure you the infection
has reached Canada. We are pushing along almost as fast as the
Yankees. What is one to do? If you don't run with the crowd,
you will soon be trampled under foot. It makes one yearn for
quiet, steady, solid Britain, where a great deal more is achieved
with a great deal less fuss and flurry than on this swift continent.

When a man is courtly and deferential to a woman nowadays we
say that he is "a gentleman of the old school." Do we mean by
that that the men of the present day are lacking in politeness to
the other sex? I'm afraid we do. Old-time gallantry and chivalry

is gradually passing away. Who has done this? Woman herself has done it because it is the fashion to pretend to meet men on equal footing.

Young women have assumed an air of independence; young men an air of indifference. Men have tacitly inferred that women scorn the sort of consideration that one time they felt was their tribute to womanhood. Politeness has become lax and the grace of homage forgotten. The highest standard of manners cannot thrive in an atmosphere charged with rivalry. Women first discovered this when they went into business and now they are discovering it in their social relations. This will grow. There can never be a return to the primitive politeness of the old days until the New Woman is dead, and there are no signs of her becoming an extinct species.

At all the quick-lunch counters frequented mostly by men, the patrons are obliged to wait on themselves. Even their cheques are not served to them. These establishments seem to have extra faith in human nature and after first letting a fellow grab what food he chooses for himself he is allowed to add up what he owes and hand the money over to the cashier, who takes his word for it. But notwithstanding the implicit trust of it all, the man does all the work. He works hard too for it's no sinecure grabbing those dishes and serving himself. What bothers me is that these same men are sure to object if they are obliged to do anything for themselves at home. How they insist on being served just so! When house-cleaning time comes around or there is a domestic interregnum of any sort, how aggrieved a man is at having to put up with paltry table service and how righteously indignant he is if obliged to do with makeshifts. And then this same man will go into a quick-lunch counter and hustle around as if his life depended on it, and all so tamely, willingly, almost humbly.

Now that it is very much the fashion to be old-fashioned in the matters of house-furnishing some curious phases of behavior are revealed. First among these comes the shrewdness of the dealers in putting a high price upon any article because it happens to be old and in working it off upon their gullible patrons when it has neither value nor beauty to recommend it. The antiquity shops of rural regions are replete with this kind of thing. The few articles to be found there of the slightest intrinsic worth are sure to be too disabled for use; the larger part of the stock never did have any value, and never can, save for the fictitious value of price and age. Moth-eaten, no-account garments, battered kitchen utensils and inartistic mantel and "what-not" ornaments —really it is pitiful to see with what eagerness people put good money into the purchase of such trophies.

"My grandmother has a set of purple and white dinner china that belonged to her mother," said a woman visiting an antiquity shop. "For years I have considered it the ugliest set of dinner china on earth. It is so hideous that all of us children and grandchildren have let it be known that its bequest would be regarded as an insult. At an antiquity shop in the town where I spent my summer, the star piece of the collection was a lidless, handleless sugar-bowl of the precise pattern and color of my grandmother's despised dishes. For this sugar-bowl they asked $10. I'm now praying that my grandmother will leave it all to me so that I can make a fortune selling it piece by piece." As far as I can see, the stock-in-trade of country antiquity shops consists of all the old things which we've all been trying to get rid of for years.

Having a telephone in your house has many advantages, but also it has disadvantages. Women who keep a telephone no longer do their own marketing. There is no choosing of your steak, your roast, your poultry. You leave the furnishing of your table entirely in the hands of the tradesmen, who practically can send you what they like. Another feature of the telephone is it keeps women in the house when they would be out and about in the morning hours. It is the friend of obesity, laziness and thriftlessness, and very often a distinct source of annoyance from a social point of view. And yet we would feel crippled without it, though in reality it is an intruder in the privacy of the home, and it is an impolite medium of conversation, and worse than ten women in the matter of diffusing gossip.

The Cinematographe is too good a thing to let run away from us. It is a large factor in education. It ought to be subsidized by the government and offered as a free spectacle to the public. What it may do for the world in the future in preserving for us the great ones who pass so swiftly into the Silent Land is invaluable. Who, ten, twenty, fifty years from now, would not look with delight at a moving picture of Gladstone in the act of delivering a speech? It is the hope of everyone who sees this wonderful photographic invention that it will be used to cheat death by preserving the features and actions of the great ones.

The latest French invention is a talking watch. A tiny phonograph is applied to the timekeeper so that when you touch a spring a voice tells you the time of day. How weird to hear that small voice speaking in the watches of the night. A talking watch would be worse than a conscience.

The owner of a country house, shortly after the golf links were laid out, lined up his daughters before him and announced that he had something to say. "Now girls, I want you to learn golf, but you must golf right. No standing around and posing and letting others do the work for you. You must lug your own tees and clubs and run after your own balls. You must carry your own hats too, or leave them behind."

The girls were somewhat appalled, but they wanted to golf so they undertook it even under the conditions imposed by their father. "I don't like it one bit," frankly confessed one of the girls. "Golf is all right but this independent, every-girl-for-herself golf —well, it soils my hands and bending over makes my back ache. Half the fun of a girl's doing anything is having someone else to do it for her."

"I'm no strong-minded woman's rightster," announced another girl. "I'm a clinging-vine type. This having to take care of yourself is no fun. I don't want to vote or wear trousers nor speak in public or anything else a clinging-vine wouldn't do." The question is, what was the parental objective in making the girls be independent? Well, the wise father knew that if the girls had played "clinging-vine" style they would have hungered for independence, for asserting themselves. That father chose a smart way (in golf or anything else) to keep his daughters from developing into New Women.

I heard of a girl this week who had come to the conclusion that domestic work was not genteel enough for her and therefore she had decided to seek work in a store. She was a good servant but she had what she supposed were higher ambitions. Just as you will find a few native American servants, so our young women are beginning to loathe the kitchen, to up-tilt their noses at any connection with pots and pans. It would seem that ultimately we shall have to do without domestic servants. Under the circumstances, I think there is room for an organization to supply help at so much an hour. If one could telephone a bureau for a cook for half a day, a scrublady for a few hours, it might be possible to exist. The big demand would be for wash-up ladies. They would have to be delivered on special street cars. Perhaps, however, in the future we shall have our dinners delivered, ready-cooked, by van, the crocks and cutlery to be called for an hour or two later. Fancy the peace and rest this would give the weary housekeeper.

The safe which was blown open by bank robbers at Bowmanville a week since was made twenty-three or twenty-four years ago. At that time it was an up-to-date two-combination concern, the best and the stoutest of its kind. Today, so vast have been the improvements in safe-making, it would seem but a scant production beside the solid, mighty machines armed with innumerable locks, bolts, wheels, combinations, time-clocks, and rubber packing that are turned out week after week by the large safe factories.

A game is being continually played by the safe-makers. On one side of the board sits the manufacturers; scientific, inventive, restlessly discovering; on the other side are the Fire Demon and the Burglar. Two to one. Now one side, and now the other, cries "Check!" It is a microcosm of that duel in armour plates and guns that is continually being played by nations. Oak ships. Thirty-two pounders. Four-inch armour plates. Heavy guns with conical steel balls. Six-inch armour plates of Harveyized steel. Heavier guns and harder projectiles. So it is with the safe-makers. Mild steel doors. Drills and gunpowder. Hardened steel doors. Nitro-glycerine. Rubber joints and packing to the doors to prevent nitro-glycerine being poured in. "Check!" cry the safe-makers. And now the burglars sit, cautious and determined, trying to figure out how to open safes that are proof against nitroglycerine.

The great Toronto safe works rears its many-windowed cube down where the haycarts come in from the country. Here, close by the fragrant result of rural toil and simplicity, sits one of the players in this game between Science and Crime. We peered through the gloom of the mighty workshop inside. A blue haze wreathed and clung to the roof and circled slowly about the figures of the men at work and the many machines, cutting, snipping, punching, laboring like vital things beside the human figures that look so small but whose slaves and henchmen they are. The noise is thunderous. Everything seems to be stewing in a huge cauldron. Far down the vast chamber the red glow of forges throws lurid light; all about are Rembrandt shadows, amid which figures move vaguely. There is no sound of human voice.

Far up in lofty places lie the workshops of the locksmiths, and the carpenters. And the decorators: in some grim irony, the safes are ornamented with fairy-like arabesques that accord quaintly with their monster strength. The burglar is complimented by having a pretty landscape to contemplate. Why not instead paint a few texts on the steel doors? "The jimmy is mightier than the sword." Then, again, "To be good is to be happy," might tempt him to seek the narrow trail of honesty.

"We've been looking for this for years," said the manager, alluding to the nitro-glycerine, "and we've got to fight it." So Science girds its loins to meet the strong sinews of Crime. "Check!" "Checkmate!" The war speeds on, quiet, tense, terrible. The great hammers beat their wishes into iron and steel—the fine cobwebby brain of the workman spins out bars and bolts and lock and rubber jacket. In his lair, watching from under bent brows, the burglar spins a fabric finer than any, laughing as he spins some fine implement, or brews some furious fluid that will send the massive bolts and locks flying in splinters, and give into his greedy hands that before which the mightiest weapon the world has ever known melts as snow before rain—gold.

Prof. Elisha Gray has solved the problem of sending your own written words, has solved perhaps the most difficult problem in applied electricity. To watch this instrument—a man writing off to one side at what is called a "transmitter," and on the other side, at a "receiver," a ghostly pen following with perfect exactness his words, reproducing them instantaneously as they are written—is to experience a weird sensation. It is like witchcraft.

The electrical impulses coming over a wire move the pen of the receiver simultaneously with the movements of the pen in the sender's hand. As the pen passes over the paper an ink tracing is left, which is a perfect facsimile of the sender's motions, and you can sketch, add a column of figures, or make any signs you like.

Once this machine is in common use there will be no more blunders such as the telegraph and telephone commit. The telautograph machine gives its message privately. A man can sign a cheque at any distance, and surely now, if ever, one can project oneself into space. The electric inventions of our times are fast binding the world in a close circle. To live in the full sense we must be in touch with the lives of others. We are on the edge of a world of new forces, at the door of a new life. These things are great because they are humanizing.

Blessed be fads, they are the crumbs the gods send to the poor journalists who grope under the Olympian dinner tables. We have had the bicycle fad, the golf fad, and countless others. Now we are presented with the fad of the Muscular Maiden. The recent notice in the press that Miss Rosa Burke has challenged all, or any of the female world, to meet her in the ring, and that that challenge has been accepted, has startled a world that should by this time be accustomed to shocks.

A tremendous cry arose at the advent of the New Woman. She was said to be a monster. She elbowed her way into the newspapers and magazines and she acquired a vogue. And now advances the Muscular Maiden. The most shocking of all the "avocations" has been seized by this latest phase of the New Woman. Rosa Burke steps forth and throws a moral dynamite bomb into the heart of society. And a gazelle, with soft, dark eyes, takes up the challenge and, in the sight of a stunned world, claims she's prepared to strip to the waist.

Now it is hardly possible to unwomanize a woman and, when it is done, it is by diabolical tricks that she is made, or makes herself, a monster. The New Woman is just a woman. Up to this time, the caperings of the New Woman have been bearable. But this newest phase is distinctly horrifying.

The Medical Girl has proved that she can more than hold her own in the profession. She has sturdily faced the horrors of anatomy—has, with eager fingers and keen scalpel, explored the body of some aged pauper, has penetrated the cerebellum of a judge, or laid bare the shapely gastro-cnemii of a right reverend—and so has earned her spurs. The Lawyer Girl understands her nisi prius and non assumpsit and has tasted the wisdom that lies in the dry dustiness of the gown that looks so dignified and grand before the jury. She, too, has been accepted—with some grumbling—but the earth revolts against the Pugilist Girl.

Some man may yearn for a muscular wife. He may care about a prettily-developed trapezium, or beautiful biceps. He may readily fall into rapture over her charming deltoid, or look forward to settling conjugal differences by putting on the gloves. Such men are rare. Yet the female prize-fighting ring looms in the future. That rib of Adam's is certainly assuming alarming purposes.

4. POLITICS AS USUAL

Kit's immense popularity was not lost on Conservative party organizer John Stoddard. Realizing that she would probably win by a landslide, he called at her home in 1898 and asked her to run in the next federal election. He was swiftly, politely, refused and when he persisted, Kit's temper flared. "I would not make a good politician," she said "because I am woefully deficient in two areas. I cannot lie and I am hopeless at stealing." Stoddard obviously was not a loyal "Woman's Kingdom" reader. If he had been, he would have known that Kit felt most politicians were either bumbling fools incapable of holding decision-making jobs in private industry or sleight-of-mouth con artists. Her low opinion was formed in her youth. Her father had engineered a triumphant campaign for a mayoralty candidate who promised to wipe out civic waste and corruption. After he was in office a few months, he was caught soliciting bribes. His avarice was extraordinary. Besides cash, he accepted clothing, furniture, and even an outdoor privy from favor-seeking constituents.

Kit did, however, admire Laurier. She wrote that he was "a person of spotless honesty" who was "so utterly charming you can't help liking him, although some of his policies are quite senseless." Yet her lofty regard for the Prime Minister did not influence her views on politicians in general. Year in, year out, she gave them a spirited thrashing. 2018787

The choice at a general election is between the devil the country knows and the devil it has partly forgotten about.

Let no one ever tell me again that it is women who make the most noise with their tongues. All the way down in the night [she

had travelled by train to Ottawa for the opening of Parliament in
1898] the voices of men buzzed and hummed and boomed
through the sleeper. Fat politicians—why are politicians nearly
all fat and fifty?—gabbled State's "secrets," then snored, then
woke, then gabbled again, and finally got up in the middle of
the night and began to whistle cheerfully. The four women travelling with them behaved decorously. Not so old Adam—he
made enough noise to turn the serpent out of Eden.

The winding sounds of politics also surge through the Ottawa
streets, the hotel corridors, the dining halls, and the elevators,
round the doors of which the crowds congregate. All kinds of
people are here with little schemes to put through. The historic
Russell House is, as usual, the Conservative rendezvous. Gay
parties gather about the small tables and there is the cheerful
sound of popping corks. The women are exploiting their newest
frocks, though the smartest of these are reserved for the drawing-room tonight.

A drab crowd of men was what one first fell into. How unin-
teresting men are, with their colorless clothes and sameness of
attire. Not a flirting feather or bright ribbon among them. All
dingy and grey. But in the ladies' parlor—that dear room into
which passing Senators and "Commons" and other gentlemen
cast interested glances—there are smart things in the way of
frocks. I recall a glorious creature, all in imperial purple and expensive hair and royal ermine. She wore a smashing hat, which
set off her profile with a saint-like halo. But her eyes were omi-
nous and her mouth had curve which were definitely not made
in Heaven.

Outside, clear, blue skies roof the big house on the hill, and
the grand architecture accentuates the personal insignificance of
the legislator, who looks so small and shrivelled as he mounts the
steps that lead to it. People are every moment arriving for "the
show"; all roads just now lead to Ottawa. Dress baskets and big
hand-boxes follow the women into the hotel corridors, and you
shudder with apprehension thinking of your modest valise with
its one evening gown and home-made hat. But consolation comes
with the thought that nobody knows you, and nobody cares, and
you are only an atom in the gay whirl of brilliant people who are
here from all parts of the Dominion.

I am glad to hear that those women who would insist on canvassing for their husbands in England have met with a political reverse and are justly relegated to their proper spheres. Indeed, the women may have spoiled whatever chances the men might have had. I would long be sorry, as they say in Ireland, to advocate that women should sit down with folded arms, but election campaigns are not the spots for self-respecting ladies. Fancy Dorothy Stanley going into hysterics, and Mrs. Cornwallis West, whose beauty has long been on the wane, gesticulating frantically to a crowd of sneering English tradesmen and assuring them that she would not be so unworthily treated in her own country. The truth is—she would.

The average politician has not yet learned the art of flattering people by letting them tell him things he already knows. He loses a vote everytime he reveals his knowledge to a citizen who has travelled miles clutching it in his mind.

Tea drinkings at the British House of Commons for ladies are to be done away with. Often have I sat watching lazy hay-laden barges go down the Thames, while I sipped and wrangled with an Irish member. No more for us, petticoated victims, are these delights. We are to be caged, like dangerous animals, behind the grating so that we can only squabble among ourselves. The Speaker will have no more of us pirouetting on the terrace. He wants the floor to himself.

After you meet an Ottawa veteran, you sometimes wonder if in the beginning God did not create three species—man, woman and politician.

Sir Wilfrid Laurier has a very fine head, expressive of intellectual force and much vigor. All the lines of his face express refinement and seem the outcome of a studious life. It is a face full of tact but lacking in power. His eyes show a depth of gentle shrewdness, and his hand is as soft as that of the Pope. You dislike to hear people abusing Mr. Laurier because you think it will hurt him so. But he meets everything with his serene smile, never changing his lounging attitude in the Commons, except to lounge a little more.

It is an old saying that a man and his wife grow like each other after they have lived many years together, and when they are in close accord their mental likeness is expressed upon their faces. If there be any truth in these assertions, President and Mrs. McKinley finely illustrate it. They are wonderfully alike, seen in profile, especially in the mouth, nose and chin. Since their marriage in 1871, they have scarcely been separated. Whenever business took him away from her, he never neglected to send her three telegrams a day—one in the morning, one at noon, a third to say "good night." A rare husband this. The woods are not full of them.

Once or twice since I became a journalist, people have offered money—one man for a write-up "on my wife's gown"—but, I assure you, journalists, venal as they are sometimes said to be, are not like politicians in this respect.

The masses care little for party politics; they rarely read a Bill when it is printed in the parliamentary news section. When elections are not in progress, you seldom hear of politics among the people. The masses are too busy wondering how they can get bread and butter. Politicians legislate and legislate. They talk themselves hoarse at meetings but they know little of the people they are legislating for, and care little, beyond their votes. As for crowds at the gatherings, the people like to be amused: they like to see the great men and cheer them. It's a cheap way of getting some fun. But the masses neither appreciate nor care about the mouthing of words which goes on at monster political meetings.

Mr. Gladstone will be eighty-seven on his next birthday. Lately his figure and even his face appear to be growing curiously smaller and attenuated. He is losing his height—growing down, as old people often do. In fact, he presents the appearance not of a man of eighty-six but of a well-preserved man of a hundred.

A man entering political life must possess certain qualities in order to assure success. He must not be too modest. He must

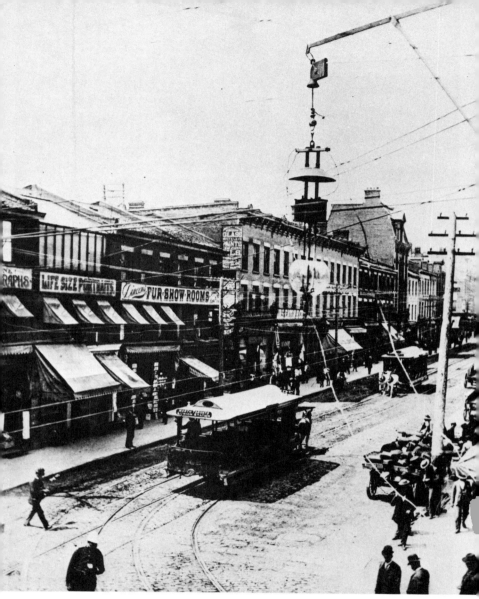

1. Yonge Street, Toronto's main thoroughfare, in the 1890s.
(Metropolitan Toronto Library Board)

2. Jarvis Street looking north from about Dundas in the 1890s. This was then one of Toronto's most desirable residential areas. (Metropolitan Toronto Library Board)

3. A downtown Toronto scene (Richmond Street West) circa 1899. (Metropolitan Toronto Library Board)

4. Lone streetcar passes by the Queen's Hotel, Front Street, circa 1894. (Ontario Archives)

5. Typical Toronto house decked out for Queen Victoria's Diamond Jubilee in July 1897. Kit traveled to London to cover the event first hand. (Metropolitan Toronto Library Board)

6. Picnic at Etobicoke Creek, 1889. (Ontario Archives)

7. Wheeling party circa 1897. (Ontario Archives)

8. Baby and carriage circa 1900. (Ontario Archives)

9. Horse-drawn delivery vans like this one were common in Toronto in the 1890s. (Ontario Archives)

After the Ball.

There is always a great rush for S. Davis & Sons' Cigars.

10. Advertisements like this one appeared frequently in the newspapers of the 1890s. (Ontario Archives)

11. Advertising was not limited to magazines and newspapers as this view of Yonge Street circa 1893 demonstrates. (Metropolitan Toronto Library Board)

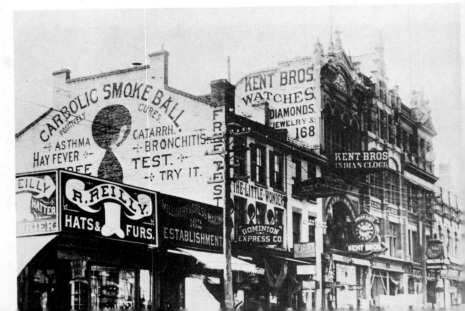

ANOTHER HOME VICTORY.

The Weak Made Strong.
The Despondent Made Joyous.

ANOTHER WONDERFUL CURE EFFECTED BY
PAINE'S CELERY COMPOUND.

Mrs. A. Acheson Suffered Intensely from Neuralgia. Rheumatism, Nervousness and Sleeplessness—Her Medical Adviser Failed to Cure—Ordinary Medicines Did Not Even Give a Measure of Relief—She Uses Paine's Celery Compound, and Says: "I am a New Woman."

12. Paine's Celery Compound, it seems, cured just about every ailment in the 1890s. There were hundreds of advertisements for the medicine, all in the style of this personal testimonial by Mrs. Albert Acheson of Montreal. (Ontario Archives)

13 and 14. The two advertisements below appeared in a program from Toronto's Princess Theatre around the turn of the century. (Metropolitan Toronto Library Board, Theatre Department)

15. Kit interviewed William Randolph Hearst during a trip to California in 1895. "Mr. Hearst's eyes are the feature which first catches your attention. . . . [They are] eyes without depth yet capable of giving you a look which pierces your very soul." (The Bettmann Archive)

16. Prime Minister Laurier was one of Kit's admirers and read her column regularly. (Ontario Archives)

learn to dissemble and probably lie (most men are well-equipped in these ways), and must make hundreds of promises he knows he will never keep and, above all, he must learn how to play on the emotions of the public. He needs humor, judgment, irony and eloquence. He must not have too many lovable qualities, or if he has them he must keep them for home, lest men call him weakly and soft. The "I" must appear often; it is a magical word in politics, and the unchecked expansion of the ego is a point of primary importance.

Ambition has little to do with political life. A tradesman trying to get into politics may desire the adulation of the crowd, his name in the papers and all that, but the great leaders would never for the mere gratification of a petty vanity have assumed the terrible burden of public life. Do you think Chamberlain cares a rap for mere public opinion, public praise or blame? Did ever the hootings of the crowd ruffle Sir John A. Macdonald or Sir Charles Tupper any more than the cheers did? Does either Mr. Laurier or Jim Sutherland care a rap about what is printed about them?

I fancy political life is forced on the men who grow to be leaders by the necessity to let their personalities develop completely. It is the haunting, ruling, dominant instinct that lies back of the heads of men which speaks and insists—from the sheer delight it will bring—on overcoming obstacles and forging to the top. A man must either rule or be ruled. The great men mount by force of will and longing for dominance, and the little men go under. Survival of the fittest makes great political leaders.

The grandson of Sir Allan Napier McNab, one of the most eminent Premiers Canada ever knew, has died at Guy's Hospital. For the last five years he lived by billiard-marking and other odd jobs. There is something melancholy in the fate of this fellow who, related to a peer, made a living at scanty jobs and died a failure. Henry McNab Davenport was born with a silver spoon in his mouth, but long before he died it turned to pewter.

They say in England the passion for the Fabians (as socialists, anarchists and labor movers are called) will pass in a season. Such a statement was actually made to me by a travelling Englishman. To be sure it was found that he hadn't read an English paper for thirteen months, and had found the North American journals "so vulgar and personal" that after one glance he had resolved not to look at one again. He knew absolutely nothing of the movement that is stirring the States of America in a struggle for rights and freedom against the terrible monopoly that is the curse of that country.

A few nights ago here in San Diego [1894] the first meeting of the Industrial Army Reserve Corps of men and women was formed. I went to see and hear these "Fabians," thinking of a remark made by the Englishman. "The real Fabian female," he said, "has no ideas and no culture. She will drink whisky when she can, as long as the male socialist will pay for it." I saw at this mass meeting hundreds of working men and women. Old men stood up to make their speeches. Strong talkings, deep and bitter they were, but there was no inciting to acts of violence or rebellion. On the contrary, they spoke always for peace and patience and unity.

The women were quiet listeners but speaking to many of them afterwards, I was met with earnest words. "We will stand by the men through it all and help as best we can. We cannot see our children hungry." The London female Fabian may be without ideas or culture; she may drink whisky and be a violent and repulsive creature, but the working woman of the States is not so. She is, nearly always, a temperance woman and, were the men to weaken, an industrial army of women would spring from every hamlet and village, and marching to Washington, D.C., would demand a cessation of the monopoly system that is ruining the country. And, somehow, I think the women would have their way.

5. SHOWTIME

The North American vaudeville circuit had its own star system. Comedians, dancers, and magicians whose names mean nothing today were collecting top dollars in the 1890s, and impresarios, competing for audiences, enticed operatic tenor Italo Campanini, soprano Nellie Melba, and actress Maud Adams onto their stages. Singer Lillian Russell's fee jumped from $35 in 1882 to $3,000 a week by 1910: her rags-to-riches career symbolized vaudeville's fast-spreading popularity, and Tony Pastor, the man who discovered that buxom beauty, is credited with launching the vaudeville phenomenon.

In October 1881, Pastor put on a show in his New York theater featuring male impersonator Ella Wesner: all of the performers were warned that they would be fired if they made crude gestures, swore, or told suggestive jokes. Pastor was out to clean up vaudeville, which had a reputation as a seedy, off-color amusement fit only for adult male spectators. After the success of his first simon-pure show, he lured respectable ladies to his theater by offering door prizes of silk dresses, sacks of potatoes, and cooked hams. Other owners followed his example, and, reborn as a medium suitable for family viewing, vaudeville soon outdrew all modes of popular entertainment, including minstrel shows, the circus, and touring musical-comedy troupes.

Kit covered vaudeville with the same passion she applied to the serious arts. And the same high standards: if performers lacked professional polish, she roasted them. She did not limit herself to straight reviews. She dropped innocuous anecdotes about vaudeville artists into her column and intriguing observations on the conduct of the fans. Nor did Kit stop at vaudeville. A circus, a boxing match, an animal exhibition—almost anything

that attempted to entertain the public qualified for inclusion in
"Woman's Kingdom."

When are the adolescent girls attending vaudeville and theatre matinees going to gather their senses? They are all but mobbing stalwart Jack Webster, while the other day a crowd of girls hissed the villain in The Silver King as that innocent man was making his way to a restaurant. O female reserve whither has thou flown! Imagine asking a strange man for his photograph, his autograph, a lock of his hair, a paring from his toe-nail. And this is virtuous Toronto! What queer, half-women, half-children, frequent the matinees. Have you observed these miniature women with their enormous pompadours, their high-heeled shoes, their saucy bird-ridden hats? There they go, holding up their skirts in one hand in imitation of the women in long clothes. Opera glass, fan, gloves all resemble the grown-ups, and judging from what my own ears have heard, the conversation of these perky midgets was much more grown-up than that of my granddame when she was eighty. Conversation, artificial, superficial, at times indecent, and almost touched with vulgarity is what one hears. Little girls are not what they used to be.

So chorus girls who have reached the age of sixty are to be pensioned. I venture to say that the pension bureau will not be too rushed, inasmuch as no practitioner of this particular branch of the theatrical arts has ever been known to own up to more than thirty-one birthdays.

Gentlemen, when you are squiring a number of dames who have not exactly come down in the last shower of youth to the theatre, be careful to choose chairs with extremely youthful numbers, for the ushers have a cruel way of shouting the latter at high pitch. Recently, a gentleman with a bevy of gaily dressed, but not too fresh ladies, was groping for his seats, and being short-sighted, he appealed to the usher for aid. "Thirty-eight to forty-three," shouted that wicked attendant, whereupon a few comments and guffaws were heard from the galleries. Each and every lady solemnly vowed within her breast that never again would she come to the theatre with such a stupid squire as the gentleman who sat staring at his programme, with his ears in a blaze.

Of course you went to see the circus and made the acquaintance of the Wild Man of Kootchipootchihokoones and the Electric Lady and the beautiful person who dressed herself in live snakes, and all the rest of the blessed fakers. We had a day of it. First came the chase after the big parade, which always eluded us. We stood for half-hours on the wrong street corners, sped round town on the street cars one after another, lost the morning in this gay manner, and lost the parade. The afternoon made up for it all, for we shed buns into those cavernous elephant mouths, and watched the seals play, and the lions pace, and drank pink lemonade, and grew "exceedingly hot." What a circus it was, with the beautiful ladies whirling like dervishes on the backs of milk-white steeds, and the gentleman in that very appropriate evening dress going the cakewalk on horseback.

Yet I find it difficult to forgive the Wild Man who comes from that exaggerated sneeze Kootchipootchihokoones. For a solid hour I was wedged against the rail, shielding an anxious chick, in an effort to see that monster. There was no going home until he condescended to pull the curtain string of his bed and gnash his teeth. Strange ticklings assailed one's nose as tears of heat trickled slowly down upon one's wilted collar. Small boys harassed one's legs with sharp and eager elbows. Fat women pressed from behind with a vigor that bid fair to precipitate you into the hairy arms of the Wild Man himself. Persons at either side of you dug viciously at your ribs in a violent effort to wrest your hard-won position from you. All of the venom of woman to woman spoke in your stolid, resisting, impenetrable attitude. Not an inch would you give.

You could hear the Wild Man rattling his chains inside his tent, and you felt that he must be munching beef sandwiches and drinking beer and winking his eye. At last the curtain was drawn aside and—the corner was dark and dim—a monstrous thing, dressed in furs, capered and leered and gnashed his false teeth at you. For a minute only. Then the curtain rang down. As for the Electric Lady, she was a shocking person who gloried in running needles and pins into you, and telling you you were highly charged with the essence of life. And, as for the young person who walked upon sword blades, I believe that her feet were cocained. How, otherwise, could they be so unfeeling?

Rosina Volkes is about finished. All week she has been dancing at Hooley's, shaking her golden wig that looks so pathetically out-of-place near her pinched, haggard face. She has frisked painfully before the footlights, turning her back to you when the shaking cough took her. She ought to be home in bed. She is too old a lady to frisk about when she has a bad illness. If she were a debutante or a passion-loved favorite of the fickle public, it would be another matter, but no one wants to see an aged lady gambol through her act.

The people want youth and beauty. Nothing but a divine talent holds the public, fascinating it by caresses, and only a genuis will be accepted as a prime favorite if she does not have youth and beauty. But a sick woman, who has never had beauty, who dresses atrociously, whose youth is a forgotten dream, and whose talent, at best, never lifted her above the first rank of sprightly comedy, is not a sight the public cares to expend its dollars on. Miss Volkes is playing her farewell week here. It is a pity that she did not go while we could remember her as buoyant. Too many players stop on the boards till the paint and the tinsel only show what dreadful wrecks they are.

We fancied that the older a country gets the finer, more cultured it would become. That we are altogether behind the times in our ideas is accurately proved by the swing of the world's pendulum towards ruffianism instead of refinement. The mad enthusiasm over the Mitchell-Corbett fight proves this. Every saying, every action of the winner of the fight is recorded with loving minuteness in the journals devoted to sports. One gentleman [world heavyweight champion James J. Corbett] who is received by thousands of enthusiasts at every railway station where he stops expresses his willingness to "lick any man in the crowd," if that deluded person will let him; hence he is regarded with love and reverence by all men and some women. He has not yet slaughtered any fellow creature but that delightful forbearance probably arises from the fact that anxious attendants prevent him,

fearing the loss of a large purse. Still, denizens of club and saloon believe that he can kill any man with a blow and thus a
halo of mystery and terror surrounds him.

The champion travels from town to town and his progress is
almost royal in magnificence. When he arrives at a destination, he
is met by a dense multitude. He proceeds to his hotel in a carriage amid the clamorous adulation of the assembled fools. His
presence seems to disorganize society. And money is spilled like
water by the 'sports' mad to watch two men pound each other
into shapelessness. I think the publication of a plain description
giving surgical details of what occurs would effectively prevent
really refined people from passively lending their countenance to
prize fighting. They would rise and banish the horror from their
midst.

What an ennobling spectacle that fight the other night must
have been! How soul-raising to see one fellow maul the other
until, in the sweetly poetic phrases of the fraternity, he was "sent
to sleep." How "beautiful" that third round must have been
when, dazed and giddy, one staggering bruiser stood up for
"punishment" and the other "gentleman" administered it. Mr.
Corbett has nothing to be proud of in that last blow of his. A
lesser one would have gained his end, and would have assured
us that he had some claim to his title of "Gentleman Jim." And
think of the precious creatures who are glorying over it all. They
do not suffer any pain or shame themselves. They sit in the stalls
and watch with crazy delight a blow go home that sets a man's
teeth rattling.

There is something amazingly sad in comparing the different
ways men earn money. Take Mr. Gladstone. The welfare of one-
fourth of the world's population depends on him; if he escapes
with seventeen hours' steady labor, he counts himself fortunate.
No Roman Emperor ever had such a burden imposed on him as
the Prime Minister of Great Britain, and the exalted State servant is paid £5,000 a year—exactly the amount Mr. Corbett
"knocked out" of his man in nine minutes by flapping him about
the head with leather pads!

Col. William F. Cody ("Buffalo Bill") tells of a dog that travels
with his show—a dog that is a most ill-tempered beast. The

Colonel says: "He sleeps in the ticket waggon. Every night before he is shut up the ticket seller gives him a bone, which he promptly conceals in a hole dug beneath the waggon. Failing to realize that almost every night the waggon is shifted on the road, he can't understand why his morning's search for the bone is futile. Then he's mad. He thinks someone's stolen it and you can't go near him for hours. He's planted bones all over North America and Europe, and has lost ninety-nine out of a hundred."

I thoroughly agree with my friend "Mack" of *Saturday Night* in his criticism of the National History Exhibit. The building is narrow, shabby and none too clean. The fish exhibits are repulsive, and the stuffed birds have a tired air, as though they have done this sort of thing once too often and would like a rest. The caged eagle was a depressing sight when one remembered what liberty means to a bold, fearless creature like him. Were he mine he would have sailed away from city places till he found a lonely cliff. As for the porcupine, he did not enlist one's sympathy. He was a mere bundle of quills. And yet, maybe he too had dreams.

Shea's vaudeville theatre is resplendent in stars. There is not a poor feature on the programme. Particularly to be recommended is the marvellous performance of the pretty girl Florizell, who takes desperate liberties with her skeleton. She appears to be a boneless young person who can fold herself into as many pleats as a camel. Lillian Green, a well-bred girl wearing a charming gown, whistles extremely well. But the Elinore Sisters! Long will the vision of the younger Elinore lurk in my mind. She is a being for whom all men sigh in vain. Her beauty, her grace, her elegance of costume, and, above all, her tiny Trilbys and graceful gloves, are things never to be forgotten. She is an immensely clever girl and she keeps the house laughing. The Deonso Brothers do weird things with barrels and cigar boxes, while George Fuller Golden is an extraordinary monologuist. Everything at Shea's is first-class this week.

Animal-trainers invariably tell you that the beasts they train perform their antics in public "solely by kindness." Why then do the animals shrink and cower and watch with pathetically anxious eyes every movement of their master? When a dog or monkey is called upon to do something, you will catch a moment's shivering, the cowed look, the fear. Why is it that when the trainer goes to pat affectionately the dog or monkey who has done some feat the creature shrinks back? It looks as though he expects a blow.

If the animals are trained by love and gentleness why don't they come joyfully to the doing of their tricks? And the tricks themselves—how pitiful they are. Fancy a dog turning twenty-four somersaults, or walking on his front paws, or a monkey jumping a height a man would shrink from. One invariably thinks of the discomforts of the poor dumb brutes and the wretched time they must have learning to distort themselves out of all natural lines. I would find it difficult, uncomfortable and ungraceful to walk up King Street on all fours; a dog must find it equally uncomfortable to uphold his quivering body on two legs and stagger along in an upright position. Exhibition of trained animals should be forbidden in this age of progress.

When Madame Melba is on tour she always has her letters addressed to her at the post office and calls for them herself. Recently she did so in less rich attire than she generally uses—in fact, she looked shabby. The young lady at the desk rejected the notion that this shabbily-dressed person was the divine Melba. Raising her veil, Melba sang a portion of the jewel song from Faust. The post office maiden handed over the letters and the divine one bowed, thanked her, and went out.

The scandalous treatment the citizens of Toronto received over the sale of the Irving-Terry tickets is still the leading topic with many people. If such occurred in any semi-civilized town out West it would have been considered bad enough. But here, in a city as cultured as any upon the whole continent, it was nothing short of monstrous. Toronto is large enough to fill theatrical houses when stars come to them for a week or a fortnight. To give such a population as this city boasts of the meagerment of having Henry Irving and Ellen Terry with us for three performances shows very bad management. But to allow tickets to be put up for auction, to raise prices so abnormally, deserves the sharpest censure. The local management was to blame, and people next time had better remember Mr. Irving's advice—"Don't go."

Sims Reeves is at it again. I last heard him in the Albert Hall in London, where he sang with Patti, Edward Lloyd and Santley, and his old voice was sweet and clear. Now he has given another "farewell" concert—he's been "farewelling" for a number of years —to help provide his necessities. A man who has sung before crowned heads and at concerts is being obliged, at seventy, to quaver out the ballads which long ago made him famous. It was pathetic, the London papers said, to see him on the platform singing for his mere maintenance. Hopefully, England will not permit this father of song to drift to the workhouse as so many of her splendid sons and daughters have drifted when their sun was set.

Somebody grumbles at melodrama through seven sheets of letter paper. "There is no real stage art in Toronto these days. We are forced to put up with melodrama that could drive one melancholy mad. Do say something in your column to decry this stage decadence. Women are the guilty ones. See them flock to second-rate theatre matinees to weep crocodile tears over Uncle Tom's Cabin."

Well, I like melodrama. The blasé young man about town, the Anglo-maniac who roves at large in Canada, will put on his monocle and yawn at this expression of my ignorance. But I can endure his haughty shrug, and think what a shame it is people can't stay young enough in heart to enjoy a little of everything.

What can be better than an exciting, blood-curdling melodrama where the heroine is an angel of goodness in white muslin, and never grows a day older than sixteen, and where the villain has a heart as black as the clothes he wears? It is good to look up in the gallery and see the boy-gods, round-eyed and enthusiastic in their cheers for virtue. Virtue doesn't get a special amount of cheering off the stage, so let's have all we can inside the playhouse.

6. HEALTH AND BEAUTY

Advertisers striving to win favor with feminine buyers paid higher than usual rates to ballyhoo their products on the "Woman's Kingdom" page. Celebrities such as bandmaster John Philip Sousa ("Vin Mariani is beneficial for brain-workers and those expending nervous energy") and actress Sarah Bernhardt ("Jain's face cream brings youth to my cheeks") gave testimonials; so did a plump, middle-aged lady calling herself Kathryn of Toronto: she swore that sleeping in a black rubber mask, equipped with holes for nose and mouth, eradicated wrinkles. While the admen were pleased with "Woman's Kingdom"'s success, they often had good reason to be displeased with Kit. She was not the least bit hesitant about telling her readers that such and such a product was worthless. The admen simply gritted their teeth and continued printing their exaggerated claims. Kit took the health and beauty section of her column seriously. Not for herself—for Lord knows she never practiced any beautifying strategy—but for her readers' sake. She studied dermatology at a night school and she read whatever books on dieting and the virtues of physical exercise that she could find. Still, she had an astonishing weakness for "old wives'" remedies: if a trusted friend told her that eating live frogs could vanquish blackheads, Kit was liable to print it.

It is said that mice dung, with the ashes of burnt wasps, and hazelnuts and a touch of vinegar of roses put thereto, doth trimly deck a bald place with hairs in that place. This was the secret of a notable practiser.

The mouth is one of the most attractive parts of a woman's face and, next to her eyes, best tells observant people her character. If women are good-tempered, and cheerful, the mouth will betray them even more than their words will do. If they are disagreeable to live with, and with a temper that refuses to bear even the friendliest investigation, why, then, they will be betrayed also. Tiresome, tell-tale lines will form about the mouth when girls are young, only to graven deep into the skin as they grow older. Then they awake too late to the fact that they are branded as bad-tempered and selfish among friends.

Some of us have pretty mouths; some have the reverse. But don't think because you are blessed with a large mouth that this is any reason why it should not be attractive. Indeed, a large mouth often shows more character and good temper than the proverbial cherry kind that old-fashioned novelists treated us to for so long—the sort of mouth that was the very personification of the 'prunes and prism' recipe.

Belle S.: The craving for raw rice, tea and starch arises from an unhealthy, hysterical temperament. As a rule, men are not tempted in this manner. Try to repress it, and if it is too strong, see a doctor.

A wrinkle is apt to make a woman look serious. If you have a deep one get your chemist to mix you, of alcohol, twelve drachms; of benzoin, two drms; of storax gum, two drms; of balsam of Judea, five drms. Spread a few drops on your wrinkle and allow it to dry. Wash off in the morning with vinegar.

Country Girl: I know nothing of the electric needle beyond that once I had a tiny hair eliminated from the back of my wrist, and that it did not hurt, and left only a tiny mark that time has obliterated. I have heard that it is not too painful when used on the lip, but that is rather expensive. However, a moustache on a girl's lip does not fascinate me and, unless your suitor has a decidedly odd notion of what constitutes beauty, I'd have it removed if I were you.

A beauty is not a beauty all the world over. Women in Japan are lovely with gold teeth; those of the Indies stain their teeth red. In Greenland the women cover their faces with green and yellow pigment. In Persia an aquiline nose is a necessity to either male or female beauty, and frequently out of a family of sons the accession to the throne has been decided by the shape of the nose. Red hair is viewed with horror in Persia and always dyed. Just the opposite in Turkey where red hair is counted as great beauty and women dye their hair that color. In China, where most eyes are narrow and long, a small, round eye is considered an extraordinary beauty. Turkish women paint their eyebrows with gold (at night the effect is very odd but not displeasing), and in Spain even the youngest girls paint and powder absurdly. So perhaps the Canadian notion that having a ghostly pale face, caked in powder, is the supreme summit of beauty is not so weird. Nor, perhaps, is it weird to contemplate that the experts are now informing us that golden hair and red hair are in bad form and, to be admired, one should have dark locks. So powder your faces, ladies, and hide your natural gold or red under an ink-black toupée, and remember that you aren't the only female on earth to go to laughable extremes to pander to the tastes of the fashion rulers.

To prevent skin from growing up over the fingernails, cut a piece off a lemon and stick the nails into the freshly cut part. Two or three times a day.

Homely One: Don't fret over your ugliness. Beauty is a God gift, to be sure, and it is hard to help regretting one's own homeliness. But look at the bright side. You are free from the temptations of a beautiful woman. Do you realize what these are? The beautiful woman seldom hears truth when young; she regrets that loss when she is old. She is constantly flattered, and flattery is empty praise that is not earnest; glory of face often hides poverty of heart. My dear, let another homely woman comfort you. Time can rob you of but little; it will end the beautiful woman who depends on her beauty alone.

For inflamed or weak eyes have your chemist make up this wash: sugar of lead, five grains; sulphate of zinc, five grains; rosewater, two ounces; morphine, one grain. Bathe the eyes frequently.

The fate of beautiful Syble Saunderson, the singer, is verging on the awful. She has rendered herself fatally ill by dieting. Anxious to get thin, she drank hot water and ate next to nothing. How foolish women are to play with their constitution merely for appearance sake.

Peter Royson: You say that you are glad that I am advocating public baths for women, and that you feel women are not as particular as they might be in the matter of personal cleanliness. I must say that I agree. Every woman does not take a daily tub and, I fancy, most men do. I was shocked at a very finely-dressed young woman's ears the other day in the tram. They were so black inside that if given a small spade and some seed one might grow flowers in them. She had on a silk blouse and her hair was beautifully crimped and her collar irreproachable; but, oh, those awful ears! I met a woman once (she kept a boardinghouse and charged extra for tub-washings) who expostulated because one wanted a daily wash. "It's always the way with foreigners," she said. "They must be forever scrubbing themselves. I could show you a foot that hasn't seen water for over two months, an' yet it's as white an' clean as your own." "No doubt," I said in a hurry, "but pray don't take off your shoe and stocking to show me. You might catch a cold." It seems a shocking thing to say in the face of the supposed refinement of women but, taken all round, man is the cleaner animal.

Grind mustard with vinegar and rub it hard on the palms of the hands and soles of the feet. It will help forgetful persons.

Take a pint of white wine, one handful of woodbine leaves, or two or three ounces of water of woodbine, and a quarter of a pound of powder of ginger; seethe them together until they be thick, and anoint a red-pimpled face therewith five or six times, and it will make it fair.

Oranges are said to make you beautiful. Eat three every day for a month or two. Your skin will be found clear and your eye sparkling, and your body will be vigorous.

If you are inclined to be stout, the experts say you must give up potatoes. What utter rot! Look at the exquisite dewy complexions, champagne eyes and slim figures of the Irish people who are brought up on spuds.

Mrs. Ayer died the other day in Paris. She was the widow of the patent medicine and complexion king, and immensely wealthy. She was an extremely old woman who never permitted herself to grow old. When her eyebrows vanished, she substituted strips of black felt. The lower part of her cheeks and throat were sustained by pieces of parchment gummed on. Enamel and poudre de riz did the rest. When a woman passes fifty, she ought to make up her mind to grow old gracefully. Any efforts towards youth after fifty are usually disastrous. Mrs. Ayer was nearly eighty when she died but she wore a light-brown wig and felt eye-brows to the last. Probably she was happy in the belief the world was deceived.

For excessive perspiration of the hands sponge with vinegar and water, one part to seven, and powder with boric acid.

The spring medicine of molasses, sulphur and cream of tartar is not good to take when the weather is cold. It is excellent during those warm, dull days—the real spring days of rain and muttering thunder. Nor should aenemic women take it at all. Weak, pale, nervous women should never dose themselves with even the most simple medicines. Here is how the medicine is made up. To a pint of molasses add three ounces of flowers of sulphur and one ounce of cream of tartar. Blend well, and take before breakfast for three mornings, one tablespoon. Stop for the next four mornings, begin again for three more, and so on during April and May. This purifies the blood and is excellent for the complexion.

The shampoo for blonde, not bleached, hair is: One oz. rhubarb stalks, one oz. strained honey. Steep in three oz. of white wine for twenty-four hours. Strain, wet the head and hair well, let it dry on; then wash the hair in clear water. This keeps the blonde tint and even restores it.

For dark and greying hair. First remember that hair once grey can only be restored by using a dye. The greying hair, however, may be prevented by using sage tea. Take a handful of garden sage or dried sage, make tea with boiling water, a cup to the handful. Let it get cold, strain, and wash the hair in this. Do not rinse until the next day. Use three times a week.

Sunburn is bad for the skin. If girls would realize this when they go gloriously out for the summer tanning, there would be fewer leathern faces on middle-aged ladies. Put cucumber cream on your skin before going out, wipe it off, powder well, and wear a veil. All this if you want to preserve the delicacy of the skin. If not, why, just go under the sun's rays and burn yourself brown.

Z: Diet if you wish to grow thin but why wish? When a woman gets to forty, she is better looking plump than lean. A lean and meagre old woman is not a goodly sight. Do not allow yourself to grow gross; abstain from late supper, take what exercise you can, but, above all, make beds, sweep and dust. There are no physical culture exercises which can approach these in usefulness.

Walnuts give brain food. Pine kernels serve as a substitute for bread. Green water grapes are blood purifying. Lemons and tomatoes should not be used daily in cold weather. (They have a thinning and cooling effect.) Raisins are stimulating in proportion to their quality.

Don't despise the humble lemon. With the juice of a lemon and the beaten white of an egg, milady, brush in hand, may touch up (and help remove) freckles in the seclusion of her boudoir, and no one be the wiser.

Don't be afraid of the flesh brush or glove. Friction rouses the circulation and restores tone and color to the skin.

Don't have a shiny nose and forehead because it is warm weather. Use cologne or spirits of camphor in the water when bathing.

The things that you have to do to be pretty and keep pretty are, according to recent disclosures of actresses and society women, about as numerous, tedious, and sometimes disgusting as they can be. Bernhardt—blessed Sara!—says it is all the doing of le bon Dieu. I wish le bon Dieu would extend His blessings to women who are mere women, not genuises.

Lillian Russell makes herself bloom by brushing her hair well, eating the right things for her complexion, and making bright her eyes (and stout her figure) by day sleeps. Shampoo your head often, she says, and take a dose of medicine. What shampoos we would take and what tons of Epsom salts if we could arrive at the beauty of Lillian.

Calvé, that invincible, head-turning Carmen, violates all traditions. She eats and drinks what she pleases and sleeps as little or as much as she likes. Patti goes in for massages. Her maid travels steadily over each line, ironing out the creases until the woman of sixty looks about thirty. (I could not conceive of anything more revolting than to have another woman pound on my flesh but perhaps at sixty I will eagerly give my body over to anyone if they can beat away the signs of decay.)

Bernhardt won't show her forehead. She claims women reveal their age there first. I differ with her. A woman first shows that Time has been dallying with her by the droop of the cheeks, from the corner of the mouth to the ear. Then by the flabby appearance of the turtle part of her throat.

One woman makes a beauty of herself by simply holding her chin up. It gives Emma Eames that sweet, ethereal look we see in her pictures and takes away from the hatchetty look of her jaw. There is a very great deal in accentuating your points, even your ugly points, such as leanness, which is considered eye-hurting by today's standards. Yvette Guilbert knows this. She italicizes that certain quaint ugliness of hers until, to an eye jaded with a monotony of curves and contours, she becomes an enchanting piquante.

There are many more beautifully-formed women around, according to the canons of beauty, than there are ill-formed. Every other woman has well-turned, large hips, smallish feet, good shoulders, plump arms, pass-in-a-crowd face. But given the angular, no-hipped, thin-armed woman who, in an extraordinary artistic way, knows how to make the best of herself, and you get a success. She will study, design, accentuate, not only her charms of good hair, eyes, etc., but her shortcomings—her pointed knees, red hair, sharp elbows—until these become her attractions.

Isn't it strange that dandruff is thought to be the judication of debility and ill-health in women while in the sterner sex it is thought to be an indication of physical and mental strength?

7. WORKING GIRLS

In 1898 American feminist pioneer Charlotte Perkins Gilman scandalized the country by leaving her husband and publishing a best-selling book, Women and Economics, telling women how to become financially independent. Two of her proposals, the creation of day-care centers and co-operative kitchens, seemed too revolutionary to be taken seriously. But her contention that more women should invade the work force, taking over traditionally male jobs, was broadly accepted. At least by women. Most men opined that the female infiltration of the professions had already advanced too far. (At that point, there were 5,000 lady physicians, 420 dentists, and 950 journalists in the United States. Those figures signify a big gain for women, considering that in 1871, the female doctors numbered 527, the dentists 24, and the journalists 30.) The Canadian male's response was understandable: his conditioning to see womankind as a predominantly domestic species began two hundred years earlier when the French Government, desiring to make life more bearable for the New France colonizers, devised the King's Daughters scheme. Between 1662 and 1672, 900 impoverished girls were handed fat dowries and marriage contracts and shipped across the Atlantic to wed lonely settlers. Their sole function was to cook, sew, wash clothing, and manufacture children. That, more or less, was the fate of most Canadian women until the 1800s: they were housewives, dressmakers, or store clerks, or, if they sought higher wages, teachers, nurses, prostitutes, and factory hands. The Petticoat Revolt spawned legions of highly vocal feminists and their silent sisters who just wanted to get away from the kitchen stove. Kit pointed out the enormous hurdles the working women faced (such as receiving lower salaries than their

male counterparts), but, she concluded, the female invasion was,
all things considered, a healthy and timely development.

The person who is called the New Woman is making progress. I
saw her the other day perched upon a high stool, alongside the
birds of prey who swoop above the lunch counters. The birds are
businessmen and it is their long-skirted coats which droop down
like dejected wings, and sometimes their bald heads, which
makes them look like giant turkey buzzards. The New Woman
looked very natty and trim among them as she sat upright in a
trim cloth jacket and short skirt, and studied the menu before
she ordered. The men did not seem harassed or surprised by her
company. Only one man made a remark, and he said she was a
gentlemanly fellow.

There is no doubt that a revolution has taken place in the commercial world with regards to its employees. The change has
been in the employment of women to do work formerly done by
men. It is only necessary to stand on any great thoroughfare—
say that congested corner of King and Yonge Streets—and to
watch the droves of trim girls coming along on their wheels or
crowding into the street cars to be convinced that a large and
splendid sphere of work has been opened to them. Compared
with ten years ago the change is tremendous.

Schools and business colleges have been for years turning out
by the hundreds girls who are able to do typewriting and book-
keeping.

The supply and demand have reacted on each other. Twenty
years ago many commercial people wrote all their own letters, or
had them written by men clerks of responsible character. Those
were days when rush and hurry were unknown. The clerk was a
recognized institution. Typically, he was a careful man; respectable, staid, not particularly fashionable, but painstaking in all he
did; and he took pride in doing it. There may be in the heart of
old London a few such souls left but surely nowhere else in the
world.

Many of the business firms of long-standing owed much to
these industrious men. They did not get very large salaries,
Heaven knows, and their Sunday clothing was frequently shiny.

How they managed to raise large families on their meagre wages is a mystery. Where they have drifted to, what has become of them, is another. Much of their work required correctness, persistence and memory. The boss of those days was glad to decide a question by applying to the humble individual who sat on a high stool in the back office, writing in account books. Do the bosses today ask their girl clerks about the same things? A woman's head is as good as a man's, but I doubt that she is applied to in cases of commercial difficulty.

Go into a commercial house today, and you find a perfect atmosphere of girl. You can perceive the odour of Rhine violets at times, not to mention that most undesirable of scents, musk. There are feminine hats hung up within the precincts of the office. There are girls sitting on high stools at desks. Girls with their pompadoured heads—many of them full of love affairs or their next new gown. Chewing gum has been discovered stuck under the ledges of desks. It is enough to make the old clerk turn in his grave!

The chief reason that the girls are on the high stools is that they do clerkly work for lower wages than would be asked by men. This is not fair. If a woman can do as good as a man, she ought to be paid equal wages. If she cannot do the man's work, she ought not to be employed at all. The laborer is worthy of his hire. I am thinking of this as I stand waiting for my street car at the corner of King and Yonge Streets. I see the persistent procession of young women. They look happy. They have found a career.

"Be nice to women because you are a woman," is the cry. But my inexorable answer is, "Be no nicer to women who are wanting in the fulfillment of their duties than you would be to men in the same case." Take the telephone ladies. If a male voice phones, how immediate the attention, how courteous the unknown lady who responds. Let a woman use the instrument, no matter how patiently, how gently, and let the girl on the other end be a trifle "out" in temper, how generally disagreeable she can make herself. The same with the waiter girls. They will dance and smirk for a man, any kind of a man, and let you wait and starve.

"But you are a woman. Stand up for your sex." Oh, no, not

when my sex tries to make a doormat of me. The world ding-dongs for equality. Women have set the bell a-ringing, and God forbid that I should attempt to cut the rope. But, if they have equality, women must stand their share of reprimand should they violate the rules. Why should a waiter girl smirk and simper at a fool-man when a business woman is waiting, driven by business hours, for her modest meal? Why should the telephone lady keep a woman waiting till her back aches and her temper goes to pieces, while a man's voice gets instant service? If the sexes are to be equal in the commercial world, pray let the women deal as fairly by their own sex as they do by men.

Dr. Weir Mitchell has done much to prove the value of silence to women. His famous Rest Cure forbids speaking for two or three days. I have heard of a woman of fifty-three who looks no more than thirty-five, and her habit for sometime has been the Rest Cure. Once in every month she remains in bed for two days and two nights without speaking. With noiseless tread, the servants take meals to her room. She eats little, reads no letters and amuses herself with the lightest literature. Her hair is brown and glossy, her eyes pellucid, her skin smooth and unwrinkled.

To do this one must be very wealthy. What of the toilers to whom a day's illness mean lack of bread? What of the woman scrubbing on her worn knees the huge rooms of offices and public buildings? What, too, of the weary dressmaker; the girls who typewrite in offices, who stand on weary feet all day behind the counter of a stuffy shop; who work in sweatshops, in factories, amid the clashing and clanging of machinery? They have scant time for resting. No wonder your char woman of fifty-three looks her full age; no wonder the farmer's wife, working from dawn till twilight, has that look of premature age on her face. Rest! Silence! They daren't enjoy either for one hour or the whole domestic and economic machinery would go wrong.

Bitter blow the winds of Gotham. The only sign of spring is in the New York shop windows and even the rosy wax ladies in the windows, arrayed as they are in the latest breath of fashion, look purple, as though old Boreas had slipped inside for a minute and nipped them sharply on cheek and chin. The amazing shops of

Gotham are filled with everything expensive, exclusive, daring and modest, and filled with the veriest trash! The bargain sales that take one by the throat, as it were, are so beautifully, daintily illustrated by those artists of the New York advertisements. "Shirt Waists—Newest Models—Twenty-Five Cents." What sort of shirt-waist can you get for twenty-five cents? It is made of coarse lace or cheap madras, tucked, button-holed and edged with lace, and sold to you at a profit, mind you, for twenty-five cents. Yet the women actually shoal around the bargain counter, pushing, struggling, even scrapping for a place.

And God help the women who make them! You can almost see it, can't you, the gloomy, built-about top flat where for eleven hours a day women and girls pound sewing machines, their backs aching, their eyes watery and red, their pale faces dragged and trouble-worn. You can see too the room in the East-side tenement—the living room, the bedroom, all in one—and the woman, the mother of those half-clothed, half-fed children who are tucked away in a miserable makeshift called a bed—working, working, to make food and fire and clothing for those children and herself on a blouse which would retail at twenty-five cents. With these pictures in mind, go to that bargain sale and buy those shirt waists—if you can.

No woman capable of doing higher work should consent to become a man's drudge, at any man's bidding. I am not a stickler for women's rights but I am for women's pluck and independence.

Most women of today are capable of independence and are no more slaves of love than men are. The saying about love being but an incident in a man's life while it is a woman's whole existence is today utter rubbish. It would have always been rubbish if women had had the outside work they have now. The fact is women brooded over their love affairs while they pottered about the house, and where a good many girls were in one home there was not enough work there for all, while man down at his office, meeting friends and acquaintances at his midday meal, hearing the latest news, attending to his stirring business, which every day holds surprise, adventure or disappointment, forgot, save for a few tender moments, that there was a girl he loved somewhere. And that is exactly what business women, what independent girls, are doing today with regard to men.

And this, I hold, makes love all the sweeter when the two meet. There has been no time for brooding on the girl's part, for noting the slight changes of manner, for a nursed anger over something he said two days ago and has quite forgotten, for petty jealousies. They have both been absorbed in their work, and have come together fresh from the combat, and full of the healthy good humor of working people. There is no "soul-withering" here, no narrow-mindedness, no bitterness. The girl is just as cheery as the man, even if she is over thirty and unmarried. Our novelists will have to shelf their type of old maid. She is out of date and out of fashion.

Age hardly comes into the question of old-maidism these days. There was a time when girls of five-and-twenty began to have qualms. At eight-and-twenty they felt they would be left to bind their tresses all their lives. At thirty they were wondering how it was they were not feeling much older after all. At thirty-two the world had shelved them and it was whispered that they were "prim, faded old things." The younger girls shrank from them, the young matrons laughed and they, rebuffed, unpitied on every side, closed the door of their hearts against the world, poor things, and sat in the dim chamber nursing spite and envy.

Now, who does not meet capable single women of any age under five-and-forty without the thought of their relation to marriage crossing the mind? There is no more reason why they should not be married—or marry any day—than there was when they were one-and-twenty. They have not let their lives run in grooved circles; they are women who had too much practical, healthy work to be able to moon over affairs of the heart. The women of today, as well as the men, die and are eaten by the worms, but not for love. It is women of this class who are raising the ages at which women marry, and there is this about it—marriages run far better chances of being made for love and real affection than in the days when women were glad to take any man for the sake of having a house.

Of all working women, I wonder which kind are oftenest weary. There is a public outcry against "sweaters," who work girls to

death, and warehouses who employ girls to work at pant and
vest-making. That the lives of these girls are hard ones I do not
deny, but let us look at other working women whom the press
never interferes with, yet whose lives are often intolerable. Take
the female postal clerk, the hard-working provincial actress, the
governess, the shop girls who stand on their feet all day and
have to be civil; take the hospital nurse, the newspaperwoman
who has no hours and has to do double or treble work if she
wants a couple of weeks' holiday, which doesn't do her much
good because she had nearly killed herself to procure it.

Take the lady writer who does those wretched fashion articles,
and the one who writes up Society and has to flatter and toady it
and tell fat middle-aged women they look lovely in pink and
black and buckled shoes when they really look laughable; take
the haunted, dunned boarding-housekeeper who is forever trying
to tie two ends that persistently remain yards apart; and take the
harassed young housekeeper who does all her own work. Ah, the
hidden lives of some working women! How few know about the
intense pathos of their commonplace days!

There are pleasanter things that may happen to one than arriving in New York at three o'clock in the afternoon instead of eight
in the morning. When you get into a place late at night, there is
nothing to do but to jump into bed, with all your plans ready-
made for the morning; when you arrive in the early morning,
you have a full day ahead of you. But to come toddling in—our
train fairly ambled—in the middle of the afternoon, tired, cin-
dery, hungry, is not the most pleasant of experiences. However,
it is big New York and the rush of life is everywhere, and more
keenly than ever one realizes what grain of sand in the vast des-
ert each of us is.

The next morning, we rode a Broadway streetcar filled with
businessmen and a few early shoppers. What a study of diverse
humanity these cars offer. The men, for the most part, corpulent
and gross-looking, sitting silent, absorbed in their newspapers, or
staring straight before them, never rising to give a woman a seat,
absolutely indifferent, apparently, to all things and to each other.

In the corner lurks a Jew, apprehensive, talking to himself in
low mutterings; beside him sits a large, loose-limbed man with

the face of a bird; there is the disproportioned beak, the falling
away of the lower part of the facial structure, the round, small,
bird-shaped head. Further along sits a beringed gentleman in
fur-lined coat and top hat, his red neck set in a fat roll over the
back of his collar. "A Wall Street magnate," whispered someone
in a reverent voice. "A multi-millionaire who could do more dam-
age on the Stock Exchange this morning than any other man in
New York."

Now and then a pretty woman got in the car—pretty in the
pallid, heavy, languorous way that you see so much of in New
York. All big dark eyes and a red mouth and a cloud of soft
cream powder. Gowned exquisitely, with that French chic we
Britishers are said to lack so sadly. But well-dressed and pretty
as she was, not a man looked at her twice; no one offered her a
seat. On we went, a hybrid bundle of humanity, jolting and
bounding through the streets of a great city, each one as oblivi-
ous to the other's existence as though we had never each known
the griefs, pains, fleeting joys, hopes and fears that are the common lot of everyone of us.

Later, we went in the rush, between twelve and one 'clock, to
Dennett's in Park Row, to the business-girls' quick-lunch. What a
place! Below, all white and gold, and looking-glass and glitter,
and men eating madly, as though the last trumpet would sound
in a minute and every man of them wanted to get all he could
for his money out of Dennett before the final summons sounded.
Upstairs, more white and gold and looking-glass, and long tables
where girls sat, as close as sardines in a box, and ordered flimsy
lunches and ate them in a fluster. All about on the walls are
framed mottoes: "The Lord Will Provide," and "He That Hum-
bleth Himself Shall Be Exalted and He That Exalteth Himself
Shall Be Humbled." Why these mottos are inscribed on Dennett's walls is hard to imagine since nobody but such loafers as
myself has any time to read them.

Not one of those office girls was more than ten minutes
devouring her food and rushing away. Constantly two great
streams were pouring in different directions, the one out, the
other in. Many of the girls were pretty and they wore flash jew-
ellry. Sometimes that flash jewelry is exchanged for real diamonds, and then Dennett's knows the pretty girl no more; she is

lost to Park Row and the clatter of the typewriter, but if you drop in at Shanley's one night you might see her, in a poppy-laden hat and besequinned dress, eating oyster cocktails and drinking fizz with the gentleman who is accountable for the many rings that flash on her slender fingers. And a few sad years later you may perchance come upon her in the flare of gaslight, walking, up and down, up and down, a pitiful, painted, haggard creature, who would give all the wages of her sin to be the bright-faced, careless, happy girl who used to order coffee and a cut of coconut pie at Dennett's.

8. MONEY MATTERS

*It is one of the quirks of human nature that people who have lit-
tle money delight in condemning those gilded souls whose bank
accounts they would dearly love to have. Kit mined this universal trait for all it was worth. Established upper-crust bigwigs and
the scheming nouveau riche were repeatedly rebuked in
"Woman's Kingdom." So were fortune hunters, penny-squeezing
millionaires, and the indolent sons and daughters of the elite.
Kit's close-up look at the rich and powerful in her native Ireland
set her against them. But apart from a personal prejudice, she
also liked to criticize the well-heeled minority because, quite
simply, it made good copy. In fact, money itself was, she sur-
mised, a topic the public never tired of reading about. "I can say
anything at all about money," she told her friend Jean Blewett,
"and be certain that every word will be devoured."*

*This must have been especially true in the 1890s when Canada
was striving to get out of an economic slump. Soup kitchens
were common in eastern cities and it was not unusual for children, aged ten and up, to take menial jobs to fatten their families'
subsistence income. Out west, the poverty was at its worst on the
plains: new settlers, seduced by offers of free land, shivered in
sod huts and existed on potatoes, turnips, and the occasional rab-
bit. The Klondike Gold Rush brightened the decade. What Canadian did not envy the likes of Alex MacDonald, the prospector
who took $20 million in gold from a claim he had bought for a
sack of flour? As could be expected, Kit heaped scorn on the
nouveau-riche Klondikers. The Gold Rush was, she wrote, "an in-
decently-wicked manifestation of naked greed that promises to
be more devastating to Canada's moral fibre than a bubonic
plague would be to its physical entity." For those Torontonians*

with few pennies to spare, Kit's criticism was in its perverse way, a much-appreciated measure of sweet solace.

Elderly bridegrooms are the order of the day, and it seems that they can get any girl they like for a bride as long as they have money enough. The latest groom was eighty-four; the bride twenty-four. One wonders what sort of girl could link herself to so old a man. She may enjoy one advantage, however, besides wealth. In time of need, she can turn to the older and more experienced of her husband's grandchildren for guidance.

John Barton: You are in a very undignified position, John, on your knees before a sack of gold pieces. It is the sack you really want to embrace but, alas, my dear, John, the exigencies of society demand that you begin with the lady.

Once let a woman form the idea that a man is stingy and it will take him years of hard work, as well as no end of expense, to induce her to look upon him in a favorable light.

It is fun to hear a woman tell her small daughter that she must save her pennies. The woman is usually on her way to a sale when she gives this advice.

I know of few things more humiliating than to have to ask one's husband for money. I would not do it: I would rather take in washing.

The Rockefeller baby who was born March 21st [1906] is a topic of conversation. He is the third John D. and ought, by all the laws of science, to be a perfectly beautiful human being. Every pre-natal rule ever heard of was brought into play in order to affect the unborn heir to billions. His mother was dieted according to the rules of eminent French savants; pictures of beautiful children lined the walls of her boudoir, nothing which could even suggest the faintest unpleasantness was permitted in her presence; art, music, everything refined and aesthetic surrounded this woman whose son is to inherit a thousand millions squeezed out of the blood and brains of a whole nation.

Poor little pudgy face! What did it know of the tears of sweat that added drop by drop to the terrible pile—the disgraceful monopoly of that old King of the Trusts, John D. Who is it who had not contributed to the enormous wealth of that bald-headed, bewigged old man? A human army is ruled by the sceptre that will be handed down to that wailing, pink-faced child; every other baby born in the United States at the same time will grow up to pay tribute to it; every farmer's home will send its contributions, the washerwoman who boards the street car after a hard day's work will send her pennies to swell the treasury of this small human. His income will be about $50 million a year; this means something like 50 million days of toil from all the combined homes that must contribute to the Rockefeller profits.

Injured: You are quite right; these husbands are dreadful. Fancy any husband thinking for a moment that his wife has no right to spend her time and his money exactly as she pleases!

Someone tackles me over my advocacy of the power of money. Sad fool! Doth he not know that gold smooths many of the ruts of life and sets the rudest waggon on good springs? Love is King, that it is, but Money is his Prime Minister.

Asahel Bell, a well-known miser, has been found drowned. Few will mourn his loss, for even to his family he was a source of trouble. Innumerable farmers and tradesmen who fell within his grasp will rejoice that he can persecute them no more. His peculiar mode of life was brought about by disappointment in love. He was engaged to a fair maiden and on the day of the wedding she jilted him because she had found another man who could give her more money. Thereupon Bell set out to prove that he himself could be rich.

He was a typical miser. Unshaven and dirty. He fed on stale meat and scraps begged from butchers. Sometimes he slept in a hole in a cave, sometimes on the floor of what was once the country house of a prosperous man whom he had ruined. Bell tied up men in mortgages and squeezed their money and land out of them whenever the law gave him a grip.

From town to town he walked, collecting his interest from the farmers and the rent from the number of houses which he owned. His blue overalls, his jumper, his felt-topped boots, his slouched hat and his battered valise were conspicuous on the countryside. In spite of the self-inflicted hardships, the man lived to be eighty-three—far too long in the opinion of many of his clients.

Gracious! Isn't it awful? A woman recently discarded her old man because he was too confiding to the governess. The law kindly awarded her the family, two lanky girls and a hungry boy, and she nobly swaggered out of court with them. Presently she found the sum her ex-hub paid her was not enough to make both ends meet. Hubby married the bone of contention, who now flaunts it in the ex-wife's ex-carriage, while, to add to the miseries, the lanky girls are going out governing and heaping reproaches on their devoted mother's head, and the hungry boy glares at her as he goes forth in the morning with a hunk of bread and butter in his pocket to sweep out the office of some cad his father wouldn't be talking to. Moral: Though it may be a very proper thing to shunt the wicked man who runs off the marital track, it isn't good business. Bear in mind that although a woman may relinquish the sentimental, she should never lose her grip on the material.

The Sultan of Turkey, the unspeakable, unlimited Turk, hath a jewelbox which an English woman was allowed to behold in the jewel room of the Seraglio at Constantinople. What a room it must be! Golden bird-cages hang from a frescoed ceiling that is studded with jewels, and a jewelled clock is placed face downward in the bottom of each canary's home, so that the dicky-bird may dance daily upon the back of Time.

Some of the rarest gems of the collection are interwoven in embroidered texts from the Koran, done in rich velvet. One of the most valuable parasols in the world is there, a dream of white silk embroidered with gold threads, wrought at intervals with precious stones. There are necklaces galore for the houris, and Turkish pipes with jewelled bowls and jasper stems and jingling accomplishments of hanging golden coins. Fancy that old wretch having all those glorious things.

How vulgar the striving, the struggling of the newly-rich. Take the nation to the south of us, in which the worship of materiality has become a cult, the aristocracy of which is that of the dollar, and whose scriptures are bonds, and would you rather visit its millionaires, or the middle-class cultivated people? Americans do not rightly appreciate their best people because the principal American measure of value is gold, and they cannot understand any excellence that is not in some measure gilded. They have spread their gospel to such an extent that plenty of us think the excellence in literature, or art, or even religion, must have a wealthy side to it. Large editions, big prices, wealthy congregations. Of course, it is only a phase. It will pass away because it is the effect of causes that will pass away.

And yet not to be rich is to be comparatively unknown, no matter how brilliant a man's talent. Poverty is a sin the world finds it difficult to forgive. But, then, who would rather not have been a Keats than a Vanderbilt? Meantime, we must live, and gold being a god that gives power, we will run after it. As for the poets, they are still foolishly piping on the reeds of Pan—the world hears them not, having stopped its ears with nuggets of gold.

9. PEOPLE AND PLACES

When William Randolph Hearst, the twenty-four-year-old son of a wealthy senator, took over the family newspaper, the San Francisco Examiner, *in 1887 he pledged to make it the most exciting daily on the continent. His strategy was imaginative. He raided other newspaper offices to hire their best reporters and feature writers, then put them to work spinning lurid accounts of sex scandals, political skulduggery, and whatever else suited itself to sensational treatment. Rival journalists ridiculed and loathed Hearst, but the masses approved: within two years the* Examiner's *circulation doubled, and he was making plans for his eventual invasion of New York and other major centers.*

Given Hearst's notoriety, it was only natural that Kit would travel to California in 1895 to see him. Kit abhorred his tawdry journalism (and, as it turned out, Hearst himself), yet she knew the impact a Hearst interview would have on her readers. As it is in the 1970s, the cult of the personality was very much a part of the 1890s and the early 1900s. People wanted to know all they could about celebrities, be they swindlers, press barons, or the Queen of England. Because of her reputation for frankness, many personalities refused to talk to her. When a famous American actor instructed his manager to keep her away during his Toronto appearance, Kit used her maiden name and got a job backstage for a day.

Without his knowledge, she was going to do a story on how he prepared for a performance. The actor, a father of three, carried on so openly with a young, married seamstress that Kit not only waived the story, she purposely failed to mention him at all when she reviewed the play.

Kit's personality pieces were not standard interviews: instead of quoting her subjects extensively, she concentrated on her own impressions of what they were like. It was impossible, of course, for Kit to travel everywhere and to meet all of the renowned figures of her day but, like many a newspaper columnist, that did not stop her from writing biased comments about them.

William Randolph Hearst is a mystery to all men. No one has been found yet who understands him. He is spoken of as a shy, timid man. There is a form of shyness and timidity behind which lurk cruel and terrible characteristics. Hearst is, to all appearances, in manner, in voice, in dress, a gentleman, and a kindly, gentle, humorous man. He will chat freely, even gaily, with the man whom he will knife in the back the next moment should the man stand in the way of one of his plans. I met Mr. Hearst in San Francisco. He was affable, full of humor, a lover of music and the arts.

In appearance, very tall and slender with shoulders that slope excessively. Mr. Hearst's eyes are the feature which first catch your attention. Set close together, drooping at the outer corners, they give the whole face a sinister aspect. Pale, blue eyes, surrounded by a network of tiny wrinkles, eyes without depth and yet capable of giving you a look which pierces you to your very soul.

His smile is elusive, vanishing almost as soon as it appears. It is like the smile of a woman who is deceiving you. But you return always to those pale, direct, cold blue eyes. You must because they are hynotic. Mr. Hearst has a sinister, dominant, powerful face and head, suggesting fearless, crushing, resistless [sic] aggression.

A great demagogue like Mr. Hearst is neither an honest nor a great journalist. His newspaper methods are Standard Oil methods. Libel suits are settled privately, for cash, no public apology is printed and any man or woman who has been lampooned in his *New York Journal,* or any other Hearst paper, remains still the laughed-at or execrated scoundrel in the public mind.

Mr. Hearst maintains that since the magazines use fiction, newspapers have the same right. The skeleton in every closet is dragged out to amuse or shock the public. When the records are not forthcoming the imagination of highly-paid feature editors are called upon. Mr. Hearst has bought up the maddest imaginations on the market today. He would have had Edgar Allan Poe on his staff.

Mr. Hearst claims to be the friend of the working man so he provides him and his family with the worst kind of reading. Take last week's Sunday edition. Under big headlines is related the horrid story of how the nurse girl, Jennie Ruth Burch, murdered a baby before the eyes of its mother. We have Jennie pictured as a beautiful young girl with an angel's face. She is feeding the baby with pieces of a poisoned peach while the unknowing mother sits nearby. And on the next page: "Cut Up Seven of His Wives in Little Pieces." The most frightful, gloating cruelty is expressed on the pictured face of the Emperor of Annam as he watches one of his four hundred wives being pulled along the floor by the hair while he raises his hatchet-like sword and prepares to cut her into mince pie.

Mr. Hearst is dangerous because he is inciting the poor against those who are a little better off. He is a revolution-maker. He says his ideals are Alexander, Caesar and Napoleon—and he imagines that he is all three summed up in one man.

The Countess de Castellane, once Anna Gould of New York, is now awaiting the decree that will forever separate her from her frivolous and empty-headed husband. Americans seem to be delighted that the daughter of wealthy Jay Gould has at last asserted herself. She has been patient, has endured everything, this homely, dark woman who for the love of a worthless husband completely altered her personal appearance to conform to his aesthetic ideas of beauty, but, like the worm, she has at last turned.

Beautiful, classic, unfortunate country. How the heart of the exile yearns over you. Those lonely, meagre Dublin streets; those forlorn, bleak shops; those miserable Clare cabins housing at once humans and animals. [Kit went to Ireland after covering Queen Victoria's Diamond Jubilee.] Cabins laughed at the world over, but how out-spoken, how eloquent in their appeal to all there is in pathos, pride and humor. It is the terrible blending of these three sentiments that makes the character of the Irish peasant grotesque and awful.

The "Clown of Nations" Ireland has been called. Have you ever wondered what lies under this jovial "clown"? I can tell you. The necessity for grinning when the heart is breaking; the need to laugh out loud lest the sighing of a broken soul should change the merry tune of the world's gaiety to one of melancholy; the foolish wagging of steps in a grotesque dance, lest the footsteps fall into a mournful timing to the "Dead March." The impassioned language of a million hungry people is stifled under the ringing of the fool's bell.

Industrial stagnation—that is the cause (combined with landlord absenteeism)—that is ruining Ireland. I was talking to a Drogheda carman last Sunday. "Shure everything is kilt in this countary," he said. "And why? No wan can say. But I remember a time when there was thirteen factories goin' in the town, an' now there's not wan, an' the shippin' is bad, an' the divil a thing the farmers have before them, starvation. Ireland has nothing but her religion, an' shure she'll stick to that as long as there's a blade o' green grass in her heart. She fought an' starved for it before, an' she'll do it again if she has to."

It is all very well to say, as some do, that it is her religion that has ruined Ireland, but there is this about it—no other nation has stood by the banner of Christ, fought for it, and died for it, as has this gallant country. Twenty-three evictions are this week ordered in Counties Clare and Galway, but they do not prevent the building of a new church or convent. You may say these people are fools, but you cannot accuse them of cowardice or disloyalty to their religion. They certainly have learned the beauty of the highest virtues, self-denial and self-abnegation.

An Ontario railway worker's daughter, Cassie Chadwick, was a thrice-married charmer who financed an extravagant life-style by defrauding rich Americans and banks out of an estimated $2 million. Arrested in 1905, she was in a Cleveland jail when Kit travelled south to interview her.

Kit was not alone in her desire to talk to the deceitful lady whom the Cleveland Leader *smartly dubbed "The Empress of Frenzied Finance." More than a hundred reporters had rushed to Cleveland. Championed by Hearst and Joseph Pulitzer, "yellow" journalism was flourishing throughout the continent and the Chadwick case was tailor-cut for glaring headlines. Hinting that she was the illegitimate daughter of multimillionaire Andrew Carnegie, Cassie had given diamonds and grand pianos to friends, hung paintings with pure gold frames on her walls, and reclined on couches made of sealskin and fox fur. Dinner guests ate from soup plates containing music boxes, beneath a ruby-studded chandelier, while Cassie, diamonds glittering in her hair, uttered commands to a team of servants.*

Kit haunted the city jail for days. When Cassie's attorney or anyone else who visited the fraud artist appeared, Kit and a swarming mass of reporters would pump them for information. The sheriff refused all requests for an exclusive interview. But he finally consented to letting Kit and a handful of reporters go to Cassie's comfortably furnished cell in a group. When the press delegation entered, Cassie begged the guard to take them away. He obliged. Halfway down the corridor, Kit asked if she could go back to retrieve the gloves she had left on a table. (She had dropped them there intentionally.) Returning with the guard, Kit walked into the cell to find Cassie sitting on her couch, cry-. ing. A jail matron was giving her medicine.

"How are you feeling?" Kit inquired quietly.

Not realizing Kit was a journalist, Cassie said her health had been deteriorating since her arrest. With the guard and the matron listening, fascinated, Kit sat on the couch next to the swindler and chatted amicably for over an hour. When she learned Kit was a reporter, Cassie not only continued speaking but showed her a promissory note for $5 million bearing Carnegie's forged signature: she had planned to present the note to a bank when the police arrested her. In her exclusive story, Kit called Cassie "the sharpest, boldest financier of the last century, or this," and related how she wore gold rings on "the littlest, the whitest of hands." Kit uncovered no new revelations about the Chadwick case but, instead, sketched a sympathetic picture of a misguided, suffering person. The sympathy Kit expressed for

Cassie Chadwick was not shared by the judge: she was dealt a ten-year prison term, and, her health steadily declining, she died behind bars two years later.

According to the reports that accredit Mrs. Cassie L. Chadwick with being at one time Miss Elizabeth Bigly of Woodstock, Ont., she was born of poor and uneducated parents. In her early childhood, she was of an erratic disposition. Lighthearted, gay, a merry youngster, she took the world as a football and kicked high. Granted that she is Canadian—she strenuously denies it—she went to Toledo, blossomed out as a fortune-teller, palmist, clairvoyante, under the cognomen Madame de Vere, was convicted of forgery in conjunction with one Lamb, found guilty, sentenced to ten years, let out on parole and vanished into thin air.

No more of Madame de Vere.

Later, a Mrs. Hoover married Dr. Chadwick, a well-known Cleveland physician. She settled two million dollars on him shortly after the marriage. The family consisting of Mr. Chadwick, Miss Mary Chadwick, the doctor's daughter by his first wife, Mrs. Cassie Chadwick, her son, Emil Hoover, by a former marriage, and valets, maids, etc., toured Europe and, returning to Cleveland, occupied the Chadwick mansion. The Four Hundred of Cleveland "took up" Mrs. Chadwick for a time, then dropped her. In vain Mrs. Chadwick frequented the most fashionable Methodist Church; in vain she sought to dazzle people with equipage, dress, jewels. Society women held aloft, although the husbands and brothers of society are said to have been frequent visitors to the Chadwick mansion.

The denouncement came when one Newton sued Mrs. Chadwick for a large amount. She was unable to pay it. Events crowded one upon the other. The Oberlin Bank closed. The president, Mr. Beckwith, declared his belief in Mrs. Chadwick. The moneys would all be paid in. He himself had loaned her $87,000 of his own money. Mr. Beckwith is described thus: a miser, always close-fisted and mean. Children used to run after him calling, "Miser, miser Beckwith." A bonus that Mrs. Chadwick offered was the bait that hooked President Beckwith.

Quiet, almost humble supplications are said to be the methods by which Mrs. Chadwick cozened the dollars from the coffers of close-fisted financial magnates. There are stories of immorality and blackmail. These are hardly credible. I prefer to believe that this woman "worked" the big financiers through their credulity. Mrs. Chadwick is, to my mind, too big-brained a woman to try merely sex artifices which are common to any woman who will stoop to them. She worked through the head, not the heart. The stories about her—such as she filled her house with pretty French dancing girls—are altogether too silly. Mrs. Chadwick was, or is, a financial Napoleon who would trample on nearly any sentiment in her effort to obtain the supremacy that money can bring.

This daughter of a laborer, with the brain of a Rothschild, without the money of one, played a game that stirred the world, threw trumps that made her opponents sit up, won more than one rubber, and then threw up a hand that was too daring to attempt to hold. And today, lying in Cleveland jail, she is the most humiliated woman in the world. Humiliated because she can bear anything but the word—beaten!

A thousand traits betray her. She is sympathetic if she would dare admit it. She passionately loves the big, uncouth, ugly boy of nineteen who called her, so lovingly, "Mother." Somehow that sacred word fences her about with dignity and reverence. A shell-crust is around the woman in her. Mrs. Chadwick distrusts, as do so many women whose names will never be in the paper, her one-time nearest "friends." This mentally big, powerful prisoner of the United States absolutely dreads the sight of a woman. Why? Because the weapons that women use on one another have pierced her many and many a time.

Mrs. Chadwick is beloved, deeply and earnestly, by some persons. Her son—the affection between the two is passionate, absorbing—her French maid, her Swiss massage woman, her stepdaughter, and possibly her husband. Outside of these persons, I do not believe there is one human being who has other than a harsh word or unkind thought for the woman. And yet Mrs. Chadwick has very generously given to those poorer than herself. True, she may have given Other People's Money, but she might have held such money for her own gratification.

There is much of the deep and loving qualities of femininity in Mrs. Chadwick. I, myself, in the course of a long interview, have seen the glow of motherhood, of womanhood, on a face that if hardened in the battle of life is yet capable of the fine, natural emotions. That the woman was a swindler makes small difference. She had the brains to be what most of us could not, fortunately for us. Warped desires, warped ambitions, but at least warm, human, and very commonplace aspirations.

Angie Stanton, the police matron in charge of Mrs. Chadwick, gave some details of her daily routine. "Mrs. Chadwick is in a nervous state and has frequent fainting spells. She lies mostly all day on a couch, covered with a padded silk dressing gown. She reads the papers continually, and whenever anyone comes up she covers her face with a paper. She dislikes reporters, and says they have told foolish stories about her."

"She has given largely to charity, I understand?"

"Yes. Just to give you an instance—today, when she was ordering her dinner [a restaurant delivered her meals], Fanny, an insane girl we have here, kept on saying, 'I'd like that,' and Mrs. Chadwick ordered everything she wanted."

"There is good in everyone, Miss Stanton?"

"There is lots of good in Mrs. Chadwick."

One of the first things that strikes one about the West Indies is the amount of drinking that goes on. Jamaica is worse than Nova Scotia. It is astonishing to see people drink ardent spirits at such a rate in this hot climate. Much sickness results from it. Men who drink heavily grow careless and expose themselves to the night air without taking a few precautions, like covering their heads and being careful to keep their feet from the damp of the heavy dews. These people take a chill, then comes the fever. The "bloomin'" hot climate gets the blame for the disgusting excesses of men who spend all their days and half their nights boozing in a barroom.

Up on a lofty hill stands the old church of Tijuana. A decayed and rude place with, inside, its floors of earth, its crude wooden stations and altars, a hundred years old or more. It might be a thousand in its decay and shabbiness, this shrunken and lean church. Below the hill, next to the customs-house, comes the post office, where everyone buys a ten-cent sheet of paper and writes a few lines to those at home, and then we all go into the curio shops in this town of three hundred and fifty souls, where we buy ridiculous trifles we shall never be able to carry across a continent. Gay Navajo blankets, bits of pottery, Mexican trinkets of all kinds, which one could buy far cheaper up in San Francisco. We march out with our purchases, walking boldly past the customs-house. There is no talk of duty. Either the Mexican government, with its usual laziness, overlooks such matters or the official who should be attending to them is off-duty. Storing our parcels on the bus, we further explore this forgotten, curious little town.

The principal buildings are the saloon and the restaurant, where one may taste several queer dishes. Brown children sit in the doorways, digging their toes in the sand, while their mothers, gossiping nearby, stare stolidly at us, no smile lighting their dark half-Indian faces. The entire population swarms on the streets, for this small town lives but for an hour or so every day—the time the tourist train arrives. After that it goes to sleep again, waking up only for an hour or so the next day.

In July 1897, Kit went to England for Queen Victoria's Diamond Jubilee fete. Given a meager expense account, she had to rent a cheap room in a dreary East End London boardinghouse. Informed that the famous columnist was in town, Prime Minister Laurier invited Kit to accompany him to a Buckingham Palace ceremony at which colonial troops would receive medals from the Prince of Wales. Kit ironed her dowdy dress, cleaned her shoes, and purchased a brightly colored parasol. When Laurier and his wife pulled up in front of the boardinghouse in a resplendent royal carriage, the neighbors were astonished. Gaping people gathered on the sidewalk and leaned out of windows; two dustmen, beer glasses in hand, stood in a pub doorway. Kit came gliding from her gloomy lodgings, twirling the parasol, and climbed into the carriage. She said afterward that the medal presentation ceremony was considerably less fun than witnessing the looks on the East Enders' faces.

If the good people of London Town slept at all the night before Jubilee Day they must have done it in short snatches taken mostly in the streets. All night long London hummed with sound. Hammers knocking dismally woke one up suddenly. Bands of singers went by, shouting lustily songs of war and loyalty. Now and again a woman's shriek broke across the other noises of the night, and, occasionally, the sharp wail of a child sent its whimper straight to your heart.

The dull humming of the city went on through the night like the low growling of some threatening beast, and always the hammers knocked and the saws bit their way through planks, and the night cabs crawled by the kerbs, and the strange human nighthawks flitted through the great city. Five and six o'clock saw everyone up on Jubilee morning for the Queen's parade, and in the hotels richly-dressed women, unused to such intemperate risings, made eager demands for early tea and toast, while outside the early coffee-shops were already doing a roaring business.

Down the Strand a stream of people poured. Some with tickets in their hands looking for the numbers of their boxes and their seats. Vehicular traffic was stopped at an early hour, so by eight o'clock most people were in their places. We had secured splendid seats in the Strand, where the street was narrowest; we chose them there rather than in broader thoroughfares because we wanted the mists of history and romance to fall upon us; we liked to think of all the Coronation processions that had passed this way through the ages. There was not a moment's boredom during the long wait. What with the shifting crowds on the street to observe there was no reason to be bored.

Suddenly, so suddenly that a silence fell upon the crowd, the sounds of bugling cut sharply across the air. Far-off, the thud of drums. Nearer and nearer, till the roll grew distinct, and "Rule Britannia" swept merrily down the street. Then a loud, deep cheer for here are the bluejackets, marching eight abreast, their rifles at their sides, their sailor hats cocked, and their sailor collars spread upon their goodly shoulders.

The cheers increased a thousandfold when the carriage containing Mr. and Madame Laurier passed. Our Premier certainly looked in splendid form as he bowed from side to side with courtly grace. He is the best-looking and youngest of all the colonial Premiers and his fine manners and speeches have made him a favorite here. He received a perfect ovation, and we cheered for the honor of Canada until our voice failed us.

Then came the Premiers of New South Wales, Victoria, New Zealand, Queensland, Cape Colony, Newfoundland, Tasmania and Western Australia, escorted by their troops. When the colonials passed on their way to St. Paul's, the magnificent procession of British troops began.

Wild cheers, and then silence fell for a moment, as the first pair of cream horses showed their noses down the street. The Queen was coming! Slowly the carriage carrying her Majesty drew into full sight. The eight cream-colored horses were heavily-caparisoned in crimson trappings wrought in gold. The gorgeous coachman, in white wig, red coat and heliotrope silk stockings, held the eye for a moment, and then we saw the face of the Queen, and everything else vanished.

The Queen sat alone, facing the horses. Opposite to her sat the Princess of Wales and Princess Christian. Her Majesty carried a small sunshade, the other ladies did not, but most unselfishly they faced the brilliant sunlight so that the people might have a full view of the great and good woman who so long has reigned over them. The Queen was dressed in black silk, embroidered with silver. Her black lace bonnet was trimmed with a wreath of white acacia, among which diamonds glittered. There was a touch of sadness in her Majesty's benignant face. She is far and away handsomer than any late picture I have seen of her represents her. She seemed deeply touched by the loyalty—the adoration, I might say, of her people.

A grave, somewhat serious face, one seamed by grief and pain, and yet full of benevolence, of dignity, of sympathy. It might be the Queen's last public procession and perhaps that thought came to her. For a moment her head bent slightly and the hand that held the sunshade wavered. Then that wise, gentle, benignant face turned once more to the people and the cheers that broke in a storm from British throats was the greatest sound I ever heard in my life.

Undoubtedly, study makes a difference in the expression and the pose of the head: it develops certain qualities—observation, perception, etc. Still no amount of thought or study will increase the size and weight of the brain substance. A large head and high forehead may be possessed by a perfectly stupid man. The cleverest man I ever knew, a brilliant orator, a profound thinker, a humorist whose undercurrent was sadness, had a forehead as low as a monkey's.

Disraeli, the mighty Jew, had a small head. Robert Louis Stevenson had a head no bigger than a baby's. Charles Reade's head was very small, and the largest fool, out of an idiot asylum, I ever met had a head no bigger than Tom Thumb's. On the big head side, Napoleon, Cuvier and other powerful men; Gladstone has a big head. It is simply a matter of brains, not head, and quality of brains at that.

The Royal family has dreadful taste in furnishing their palaces. The Queen's drawing-room at Balmoral is absolutely frightful, draped with that nightmare combination of colors called the Victoria tartan. Can you imagine anything more hideous than walls and windows hung with tartan? The Princess of Wales, correct as her taste in dress is, uses the most garish colors in Marlborough House. Red and crimsons, which swear at one another, are to be seen everywhere. However, such grand people can afford to do as they please.

There was no air of mystery about the stocky man who admitted you at Madam's door and gave you a pink card whereupon were printed her virtues. [Kit was visiting the salon of a renowned fortuneteller, the White Mahatma, whom she hoped to expose as a fraud.] He was uncompromisingly vulgar. You were shown into a parlor and told to wait your turn. A shabby, fly-blown room, packed with men and women. One wondered what brought the faded old creature in black to have her fortune read. The past could not have been pleasant or she would not have been looking so careworn and sad; and the future, what could it hold for a woman of sixty who had apparently failed at everything? Yet she looked at the folding doors which divided us from the White Mahatma as eagerly as any of us. Young girls were waiting too, full of giggles; staid old maidens in mittens studied Madam's achievements on the pink cards; and men leaned forward in their chairs and bit at the pieces of pasteboard.

A stout man tip-toed over to me. Why he walked on the ends of his toes and why he and everybody else spoke in whispers, it was hard to make out. But we did. The stout man bent forward confidently. "Is she any good?" he inquired. "I don't know. I'm going one before you." "Will you tell me if she's good after you're through? I'm playing her for the races. If she don't give me a straight tip, I'll tell every friend I've got and spoil her business. I guess it's love troubles you've got."

"No," I said emphatically.

"Well, speculation. No? Lost your diamonds then?"

"Never had any to lose."

"Step in, please. This way." This from the stocky man. All the women looked up nervously. The fat man winked solemnly twice and tapped his forehead with a half-chewed pink card. I followed the usher.

Into a bare room. With a table in the middle of the floor and a screen in one corner whence came odors of steak and onions. The window curtains were soiled, the few chairs were plain wood. Whence would the White Mahatma appear? From behind the screen and redolent of the juicy onion? A door behind me opened and a limp, faded, little creature walked slowly in. She might have been thirty-five or forty-five; one couldn't tell, she looked so worn and haggard. A long wrapper fell loosely about her figure.

She brought me a blank card, told me to write on it my name, age, profession, and one question. Everything was entered. Name: Jinkins. Age: sweet twenty-two. Profession: journalism. Question: Does he love me? Madam took the card (written side face-down) and sealed it in an envelope. She sat down and laid the envelope, the fastened side up, before her.

"Your name is Jinkins. I cannot tell your first name—it is not given to my mind to see. I see you surrounded by paper and pen —writing, writing—you do a lot of this work." She looked at me shrewdly. "You are younger than you look. Your age is about twenty-two, but you look many years older."

"Would you mind letting me have that envelope," I said gently.

She changed color. "I cannot do that. I would lose my impressions!"

"The back of the envelope is transparent. I know it, Madam. But don't worry, I'll pay your fee."

On my way to the door, I passed the fat man. "Is she any good?" he whispered. "Capital," I answered. May I be forgiven! But why should he not buy a bit of experience too?

A good man. That was Timothy Eaton. God's good man. There is a perfume attaching to the name of such a man not to be reached by those whom only Fame has crowned. The result of his vast business enterprises shows that, but there was something so thoroughly good, clean—one might say holy—in the whole life of the merchant prince. In an age where businessmen are apt to go to pieces and end a long life in disgrace, we should point with pride to Timothy Eaton and be fired with the desire to do as he did, to live soberly, sanely, wisely; to hold fast to a saving religious faith, letting infidelity and "free" thought, this fad and that, go by. It was a beautiful life; a beautiful death. They say he looked as one who already knew the heavenly peace and rest. He will long be mourned.

Lucie Dreyfus is not permitted to receive letters at first hand from her husband. [Captain Alfred Dreyfus, an Alsatian Jewish officer with the French General Staff, was imprisoned on Devil's Island after a prejudice-laden military court used forged evidence to convict him of treason.] She can never again behold his writing save in letters of the past that she may possess. His writing! That supreme witness that he yet lives, no matter in what agony or loneliness. Writing! A thing that emanates directly from one's thought, which is alive, part of oneself. Writing! The cause of all his disgrace and humiliation, but which still remains the last trace for her of love and broken happiness.

She must have no more of it. Any letters that arrive from I'lle du Diable are received by the Minister of Marines and Colonies, are opened, re-copied, and sent to their destination. How hard this is! Is it necessary that his wife should suffer so atrociously? Is France, land of chivalry, in danger because of a letter to a wife from a being who is completely out of the world, a being plunged for evermore in solitude, in despair, incapable now, surely, of writing any great mischief? Do the judges and ministers and lawyers know, I wonder, what a bit of writing means to a woman? Ah, what writings do we women cherish; what sacred letters, messages, words of love have we not hidden away in desks, in drawers, in corners? Foolish? Maybe. But it is the foolishness that keeps the world holy.

Were Dreyfus released tomorrow, he would doubtless be shot down on the Boulevard the moment he set foot in Paris, and the assassin would be acquitted with universal approbation. But there is no chance for Dreyfus. Guilty or innocent, he must wearily pace his terrible island, because to make public documents with which he was concerned would be to bring a war upon France.

So, knowing nothing of the way his name is stirring, not alone in France but all Europe, deaf, dumb and blind, Dreyfus paces up and down his island, silent, hopeless, apathetic. And somewhere in Paris a little woman is reading over her old love-letters with a dim eye and a breaking heart—while the world wags on its way, as full of sunshine as of tears.

England is determined to marry off Lord Kitchener. His engagement to so many different persons has been announced that he can but feel a deep admiration for the romantic spirit of the English. Talk about your sluggish Englishman indeed! Judging from the way every hero is reported into matrimonial engagements, it is safe to infer that under a cool surface the English heart is fairly bursting with love of romance. The rumor that Lord Kitchener is engaged to Miss Brown-Porter arises from the fact that she wears a locket suspended from a jewelled chain about her neck, and in the locket reposes the English hero's picture. A dangerous assumption. On that kind of hypothesis, for instance, Baden-Powell must be going to wed at least a million young ladies.

Kate Marsden, that heroic woman who has done some of the grandest work of the Red Cross Society, is under a cloud. It matters little that she has traveled 14,000 miles by sledge and tarantor and 2,000 miles by horseback through terrible Siberia in

search of a herb said to grow only in those wilds, and which was
supposed to be an absolute cure for leprosy; it matters little that
she visited, in their accursed dwelling places, the wretched creatures who seem forsaken alike by God and man; it matters little
that with her own hands she tended them. Madam Scandal has
got her grasp upon her and her good work availeth naught Kate
Marsden.

It is said to be the vile work of the Russian government, which
resented her prying into its sore places. The government declared there was never a hundred lepers in a certain province,
and Miss Marsden discovered in that same province of Ya-
kootsky several thousand afflicted ones.

The charges against Miss Marsden are wrapped in semi-mys-
tery. They are reported as being so gross in character as not to
be fit to print. Her friends—it is extraordinary how few they became!—stand by her gallantly, though it is said she has been
asked to surrender various medals and decorations, conferred
upon her by imperial and royal well-wishers. Gossip is feasting
on her dung heap, and the woman who has endured privation
and disappointment (for, having found her herb, it has proven
to be only a relief, not a cure) is slighted and cast out because
some Russians said she had fallen in love and deserted her work.

Miss Marsden strenuously denies the allegation. Broken-
hearted, she has offered to retire from her work and to give up
all the honors, if the charges are proven. Whether they are
proven or not, the shadow will always cover her name. It is the
same always—the man goes Scot free, the woman is stoned. But
not one word of this scandal do I believe of this noble woman
who has worked among the most abject of our kind. She will
wear her honors on her brave breast, I hope, till she is laid away
with them to her long rest.

17. This bicycle outfit was the height of fashion in 1894.
(Metropolitan Toronto Library Board)

GREEN BASKET CLOTH.

MOUNTAIN COSTUME.

TWO STRIKING BUT SENSIBLE COSTUMES FOR WET WEATHER.

FIGURED GRENADINE.

18, 19, 20, 21. Typical line drawings of women's fashions from the 1890s. (Ontario Archives)

HOW A COIFFURE IS BUILT.

22. Hairstyling advice from 1897. (Ontario Archives)

WHITE DUCK AND BLUE SERGE.

GINGHAM FROCK AND PIQUE
CAPE.

23, 24. Children's fashions. (Ontario Archives)

A RAINY WEATHER HAT.

AN OTTAWA BELLE.

25, 26, 27. Some hats for men and women. (Ontario Archives)

10. FICKLE FASHION

Long skirts, short skirts. Big hats, small hats. High heels, low heels. The restless shifting of the fashion wind irritated Kit so much that she remarked in her column, "I thoroughly detest fashion, and I write about its nonsensical whims solely because you ladies are so keenly interested." That was only partially true. She covered fashion trends, and carried illustrations of the newest styles on the "Woman's Kingdom" page, because the ladies liked it—and because her managing editor insisted. Whenever too many weeks passed without a fashion item, Bunting would send a terse memo imploring her to fill the gap. His devotion to the clothing trade produced the only instances when he meddled with "Woman's Kingdom"'s content. Some office wags suggested that his wife's nagging tongue prompted Bunting, a socially prominent former Conservative M.P., to prod Kit. Whatever the reason, Kit went along with his requests. It was her small concession to the man of whom she wrote, following his death in 1896, "a kinder, more liberal person never lived."

Even without Bunting, however, Kit continued to report on the latest fashions. She ridiculed some styles, vehemently defended others, and she was continually reminding the public that she believed all fashion, the good and the bad, was positively frivolous. Kit had come to realize that, whether she liked it or not, clothing trends were news and deserved periodic coverage. Indeed, the fading of the stuffy Victorian age and the emergence of the breezier Edwardian era could be seen in the length of women's dresses. When Kit launched "Woman's Kingdom" in 1889, the dress and its umpteen petticoats trailed on the ground. In the mid-1890s, bloomers and ankle skirts made an impact. By 1910, the skirt had crept up the leg, and the petticoat, once a loose-hanging symbol of modesty, clung to the hip in a most provocative manner.

To be really chic, you ought to sleep in a nightcap.

After a woman has gone through the hands of her dressmaker it will be more than ever difficult to determine which is the woman and which is—well, something else, for the new sleeves, tight almost to the shoulders, need pretty good-looking arms inside of them or they have about as much style as pump-handles.

The new hats are weird. But we say that every spring and still wear them.

Veils would be more valuable to some ladies if, in covering their faces, they closed their mouths too.

Will some wise one please invent an appliance for keeping the long skirts out of mud and dust? It gives one a cramp in the hand to hold up the thick fold of one's gown for any length of time. And they say the summer skirts will literally sweep the streets.

How often will one have to write of the horror of skinning birds alive before the average woman will make up her mind to do without a bird in her bonnet? To call women, in the face of our known cruelty, gentle or humane is simply absurd. I never see a woman with a bird in her bonnet without feeling contempt for her. I got a present of a large bunch of egrets when I was in Demerara but since I learned of the shocking way in which herons are plucked while alive I have never worn an egret.

For the life of me, I couldn't put a bird on top of my head and feel happy when I knew the creature had been tortured merely to add—by what crooked kind of reasoning this was evolved, God knows—to my personal attractiveness. Ostrich feathers are the only ones permissible in the face of this awful destruction of birds, for the ostrich is neither plucked nor killed. What fool-woman ever looked wiser or better for crowning herself with the body of an owl? If she had imbibed her brain instead of her hat, she might then have some claim to distinction.

Girls, young and old, if you have pretty ankles, you are dying to show them. Why not? Where's the sense of calling us New Women when we're wearing the fashions of our grandmothers?

A man is not in the fashion movement unless he sports a frock coat reaching nearly to his ankles. This reminds me of a lunatic with whom I once went through a quadrille set. He was a fierce-looking man, and he was all frock coat. His skirts stuck straight out whenever he danced with his partner; they got twisted around his legs and more than once I had to extricate him from yards of frock coat. It literally trailed behind him and I had to be careful about treading on the tail of it.

And here is the same kind of frock coat. A loose-flowing garment reaching to a man's heels, and he mustn't button it either. It is to be left open to all the breezes that blow, and to match it, gentlemen, you must parade the streets in wind-bag trousers. (Presently, you may have little frills around your ankles, and perhaps a hoop or two if the trousers are very wide.) It is de rigueur that you plunge one hand into the capricious pocket of your capricious trousers. Then your collars are to be higher than ever, your scarfs more waterfally than they were last season, and you won't be "in it" if you are seen without white garters. Candidly speaking, dear boys, the effect will be hideous.

How funny we women look scudding along the streets on a wet day in our long eelskin gowns. Not long ago I saw a mermaid hurrying along with her tight skirt held high in her hand, quite unconscious that at one side it was trailing and that there was a slit in her petticoat. Another woman sailed by with her gown hitched up at both sides while the train of it dipped in the mud and lashed it against her heels at every step. "How absurd," quoth I. "How ridiculous these women look." Then a small voice broke upon my musings. "There is a piece of torn petticoat trailing behind you," it said, "and it may trip you." There was a yard of silk frill wallowing in the mud. Why, the other woman was a respectable person compared to me, and the mermaid, she was a neat and aristocratic fish.

Absolutely do the wearers of the feather boa seem to think it may go on anything, suit itself to any hat or frock. The fact must be realized that the feather boa cannot fit five costumes. It is unfortunate, too, that the fashion of wearing bunches of artificial flowers should coincide with the craze for the feather boa, for what with the boa spreading itself out over the frontage, a bunch of carnations alongside, a cravat inside the boa, and a pearl necklace about the throat, the result is odiously "dressy." Being "dressy"—that is, putting too much on—is the bane of the average woman.

The gods be praised! Large feet are the fashion, and for once I am up to date!

Don't wear too many diamonds. They make eyes and teeth dull by comparison.

Apropos of the new fad of pocket-stockings—of what earthly use will they be outside of one's bedroom? The pocket is woven near the top, on the stocking, and is of some contrasting color, with a frill embroidery around it. Why all this toil over an unseen pocket, and how is one to get the street car fare? The pocket comes above and outside the knee, and no groping will discover it for you without raising your skirts, and then Inspector Archibald will, and rightly, pounce upon you, and have you up in Morality Court.

You will see women diving into doorways bound on discreet hunts after pennies for the evening paper. Our granddames wore huge pockets on their hips but over their petticoats, which were voluminous, so there was nothing indecorous in lifting one's outer skirts to get at small change. Just fancy the burst of immorality that will break over this truly moral city. By way of making himself a little popular, the Mayor ought to pass a by-law against the introduction of pocket-sockings in Toronto.

Neck-ruffs are exceedingly fashionable. The prettiest of all are pure white and of silken tulle, but very thick. Some women object that these wide neck-ruffs spoil the outline. Occasionally, there is no outline to spoil. Now that sleeves are like a second skin; that skirts are indecently tight (I think that the modern sheath skirt worn by some ultra-fashionable women is positively vulgar), it is a relief to see something at least a bit loose and fluffy, if only about the neck. But you will notice thin women wearing tighter skirts and reducing what little grace of outline a more flowing garment might give them to the level of a lamppost. Hipless women do not look natural. There is something horribly wrong with their anatomy—why do they strive to accentuate this very unpleasant fact?

Oculists have yet to be heard from concerning this new three-veil fashion, but the chances are they will condemn it. If one veil is bad for the eyes, three veils must be three times as bad. But what woman pretends to have a head for figures? That most of them have a head for veils is proved by the number that today are sporting three to a hat. First there is a veil of thinnest tulle next to the face. Then comes one of black fish-net minus the dots —dots are tabooed by smart veil-wearers. Finally comes the outer sheath in chiffon, generally grass green in color and more often thrown back as a drapery to the hat brim than used as a covering to the face. In spite of their three veils, women are usually sunburned, showing that the veils are, one and all, an unaccustomed touch, added since the return to town from summer retreats and a return to conventionality. All summer long these women probably went bare-headed. Is all the gain acquired in that way now to be counteracted by committing themselves to this triple-veil alliance?

Bloomers are the most moral dress. There can be no two opinions about it. Consider. When we women go out for an evening's junketting we strip our necks, our shoulders, our arms; we stand, sit, dance, virtually naked above the belt. Who minds it? Nobody. People say languidly, "She has a good neck." "Her shoulders are too thin." But the waltz goes on, and the man is attentive, and she is omnipotent, or thinks she is, which is the same.

Nowadays, the bicycle demands bloomers. They are the safest. They are the coming fashion. Some foolish ones, however, lately aired their opinions regarding "limbs" in the daily press. They said the reason some women were against knickers was because their lower limbs were unpresentable. As though thin legs ever prevented a girl from going on in the ballet! Anyway, there will presently dangle in our drapers' shop windows exquisitely-curved stockings, padded deftly about the middle, and tapering gently to the ankle; like the hip pads in American windows (Canada is, as yet, too modest) and the bust pads and other illusory charms. We shall all have splendid legs when bloomers really come in. We shall all have tender curves, delicious roundness, even divine angles, because we are false, everyone of us.

Nor need the men smile, with their borrowed shoulders, their padded proportions, their peaked toes, their powders and cold cream. We each defraud the other. We are liars every one. To return to bloomers. If you ask young men what they think of the innovation, they will tell you that they approve of it. "Would you care to see your sister out in them?" you ask demurely. They haw and hum and finally answer yes. "What about your sweetheart, or your wife?" Oh, no; they draw the line at sweethearts and wives. "What about your mother?" They are horrified. Mothers and elderly girls should be restrained from bloomers, they say. Let someone issue an injunction.

"No girl over 39 should be allowed to wheel. It is immoral." Unfortunately, it is the old girls who are the ardent wheelers. They love to cavort and career above the spokes, twirling and twisting in a manner that must remind them of long dead dancing days. They have descended from the shelves in myriads, and in a burst of Indian summer, are disporting themselves on the highways and by-ways. Believe me, bloomers are the most moral of garments. Ages ago, in a girlish frolic, I mind once stealing my cousin's clothes and making up as a young gentleman in them. We were walking down a country road in the moon's light. Jim—he is an Irish judge now—looked at me with disfavor. "I would never want to kiss you in a dress like that," he said. "You are not pretty. I miss the frills." I don't know if this will be the case with bloomers or no, but I cannot conceive of any poetry or romance in two seemingly-male figures wandering down a country lane. The finest chaperon in the world, bloomers. There is more deadly mischief in half an inch of lace petticoat than in forty pairs of bloomers.

Some women who have no sense of beauty or the fitness of things are wearing hoops around their arms to keep the big sleeves in shape—that is, in puffs—as all the latest blouses, when not in silk, are of diaphanous stuffs. You can see these grim skeletons under the thin material and the sight is by no means joyful.

High heels and short skirts don't agree. They are about as ill-sorted a mixture as the student of sartorics cares to view. It is a fact, though, that since the advent of the short skirt boot heels have been elevated several inches. An amazing number of the short-skirted sisters whom you meet tilt and totter along upon regular spools for heels. The bad taste of it is only paralleled by the incongruity. What's the use of going to the length, or brevity, of a dress skirt four to six inches above the ground, and then shoeing yourself in slippers or boots with high heels?

Have you bought your dog's fresh spring suit yet? Dog tailors are very busy in Paris. There is in the Galeri d'Orleans a shop where comfortable cushions are arranged before large mirrors, on which the dog stands while having his clothes tried on. Here sporting costumes, made like hunting coats, are to be had; ball costumes, masquerade dress and going-out attire are all supplied here. Dogs are provided with night-shirts too, prettily-embroidered, and actually having pocket-handkerchiefs stuck in the pockets of them. Every modish dog wears a watch, while his ladyfriend sports a jewelled collar. One day two weeks ago sixteen suicides occurred in Paris by charcoal fumes. The cause was briefly given. Poverty and hunger.

An effort is being made to dismiss the short skirt altogether, and to remain totally loyal to those long, trailing street-sweepers which are such a handicap to women. Why women should buy expensive material only to drag it around over carpets and up and down stairs, to tread on it and to tear it, is always a puzzle to the less-complex male mind. Sensible women who care about hygienic laws should never consent to wear long gowns in the street. The short skirt belongs to the breezy girl who joins you on a tramp on a frosty morning, who trudges sturdily by your side through woodlawn paths, climbing fences unaided, gathering nuts and Autumn leaves, with never a thought of the burrs she might gather in her skirt.

The short skirt belongs to the girl putting her ball on the golf links. It is the habit of the art student who sits serenely on her camp stool and sketches the impossible places from which the long skirt held her back. The short skirt belongs to the tired working girl to whom it is almost a life preserver when the weather is rainy. It even belongs to the housekeeper doing her own work with baby to be bathed and dressed, things to be carried up and down stairs, and the thousand and one bits of drudgery that come into a busy housemother's life.

The short skirt has given woman rosy cheeks, a springing step and sound health. It comes to stay. Let us hope it will never be banished—and the young man who has written this Kingdom a ream of nonsense about it promoting "wobbly" morals is to be advised to invest in a pair of blinkers.

Want to be in fashion, girls? Well, take home a hat and sit on it for five minutes, then hang it on a nail and punch it hard. After that, give it two or three more dings in front, put it on your head and play drunken man: after three falls, it will be ready to trim with four rows of lace, a·bunch of ribbon, some lilac or yellow tulips, all bunched at the back, two rows of withered cornflowers at the front, a snake's head, a bunch of grass, a bare twig, and a bird's head stuck on the crown. Then put it on and smile your sweetest at the caped youths on King Street, for you will be in the height of fashion.

There is a hint that gentlemen have at last set their faces against waiters wearing claw-hammers—in fact, duplicating gentlemen's evening dress. It is being suggested that the conventional black swallow-tails and dittoes in which waiters appear should be done away with and the color of cherubic innocence—white—should be substituted. It would be quite delightful to see our lead-footed Mercuries clad in spotless garb. Talking of men's evening dress, what a pity they cannot vary it sometimes. Why not scarlet waist-coats on occasion? As a distinguishing mark (one very necessary in some men's cases) between the gentleman and the waiter it would be invaluable.

Nothing is more atrocious than to witness a woman wearing a thick gold chain round her neck. Bracelets are also bad taste worn outdoors, yet you notice them in every tram-car on the wrists of well-dressed women whom you would expect ought to know better.

What a tyrant fashion is! Here we have the small waist and the high bust again! Everyone knows that the purgatory of many women is to be out of the fashion, but few members of the male gender realize that to be in the fashion costs many a feminine mind long-drawn-out torture. For instance, when la Mode invents a style which accentuates the grace of a tall, slim woman, she accentuates in a far greater degree the shortcomings of the short and rotund. Yet the short, plump woman who would rather perish than walk abroad in anything but the latest fashion, bows to her decree, and with an aching heart puts on the garb of slimness.

Certainly if every woman were left to her own devices in the matter of dress and style, our streets would present us with such a panorama of curious comedy as might bring a smile to the melancholy visage of an hypochondriac. It is the corset-maker, however, who rings the real changes in women. With the long, straight front the stout woman could greatly modify her unfashionable rotundity. But what is she to do now, when the curved 'spoon-bill' is here, with the small waist above it, and at top the high bust? 'Tis, forsooth, a hard problem, and the dressmakers will need a double width of Heavenly virtue to cover up with some grace the superabundance of natural charms with which some ladies are too well supplied.

The English woman puts her foot down flat when she walks, and is inclined to waddle. Your Parisienne walks much like a cat, stepping tip-toe over muddy places. The Scotch woman walks with emphasis, as if she meant to get there in spite of all obstacles. The Irish woman trails her feet after her in a lazy way and is given to shuffling. The Winnipegger walks in a careful manner, gripping the ground, even in summer, as if fearful of slipping on ice. The Toronto girl has a bit of a mince, and an occasional startled air about her, as though she were not sure where she was going. We women definitely don't walk well. But, in our high boots or high heels, it's a miracle that we walk at all.

I hate the befrilled she-shirts. Because the buttons won't button until you've raged about the room for fifteen minutes and missed your train, and because when you do get them buttoned, they won't stay so, but will keep opening and bulging out over your belt. Because, too, the laundry people charge twenty-five cents for a she-shirt and but ten or fifteen cents for a regular male shirt.

In hot weather a shirt-front decomposes too rapidly for comfort, and no woman likes to look in an advanced stage of decomposition. A wilted woman is a sad sight, and that's what a girl who started out in a stiffly-starched shirt-front in the morning looks when she gets back in the afternoon.

I used to wonder at the impatience of men whom I've seen struggling with stiff collars and fronts, but I'll never wonder again since I upset two chairs, a box of hairpins, Patsy Brannigan [Kit's pet rat] and a pitcher of hot water in a frantic endeavor to get into a pink she-shirt that burst open at the top as soon as the bottom button was fastened, and was at last flung from one side of the room to the other. If ever I get into that garment it will take scissors to get me out of it, for I will never go through what the undoing must be, seeing that getting into it is as maddening as having four teeth pulled.

There is a great deal of character in a man's moustache. As the form of the upper lip and the regions about it has largely to do with the feelings, pride, self-reliance, manliness, vanity, and other qualities that give self-control, the moustache is more particularly connected with the expression of those qualities of the reverse. When the moustache is ragged, and, as it were, flying hither and thither, there is a lack of proper self-control. When it is straight and orderly, the reverse is the case.

If there is a tendency to curl at the outer ends of the moustache there is a tendency to ambition, vanity, or display. When the curl turns upward, there is geniality, combined with a love of approbation; when the inclination is downward there is a more sedate turn of mind not unaccompanied with gloom. It is worthy of remark that good-natured men will, in playing with the moustache, invariably give it an upward inclination, whereas cross-grained or morose men will pull it obliquely downward.

Now, my friends—female, of course—look out for the twist of the moustache you love best, but do not be taken in by all these "wise saws" as to gloom, morose men, etc. One of the best men I ever knew pulled and bit his moustache in the most downward direction he could possibly get it, and the meekest man since the time of Moses, a man who was so free of vanity or pride that he was a regular doormat on whom his wife wiped her feet twenty times a day, had the most curled-up-at-the-ends, saucy-looking, come-and-kiss-me-do moustache I ever saw.

I was recently informed by a large corset-maker that men are much more fidgety over the fit of their stays than women are. Some have them sent home to try on at their leisure. They also possess a desire for prettier silks and trimmings than the fair sex. Nothing less than shimmery satin is ever looked at, while the delicate brocades obtain preference. A favorite pattern is a tiny gold or pink flower on a cream background. Apropos of corsets, I have just come across a curious story as to the origin of the corset. It was invented by a butcher during the thirteenth century as a punishment for his wife. Knowing of no practical remedy to stop her loquacity, he bethought himself of compressing her body between two vises as to almost prevent her breathing. Other husbands having gossiping wives soon followed this example, and shut their better halves up in portable prisons. The women eventually modified the corset and, incredibly, out of a barbaric instrument of punishment came an article of fashionable dress, worn equally by grand dames and women of the people.

Artificial flowers are to be worn in the hair again. I don't believe there has ever been quite so becoming a fashion for evening headdress as flowers. Rosebuds of velvet and violets of muslin are to twine around the curls of pretty girls, just above the left ear, the same as they did long ago. The red geranium is much worn in Paris and will soon be with us. I recall once at a hunt ball the prettiest girl in the room, a fair-haired West of Ireland beauty in a white gown, wore a wreath of vivid geraniums around her head, just peeping through her fringe. She was a glorious picture, the splashes of color lighting up her delicate face.

Of leagues of women there is no end. The latest is the Anti-Corset League, of which the most remarkable feature is that men are invited to join. This does not mean that the padded man who wears stays is supposed to be in need of a league to banish the corset and yet to save him from his own enormity. The real reason is that women will persist in wearing what meets with masculine approval and it is expedient to make men see the ugliness and futility of the corset. Doubtless, we can expect men to flock to the meetings—public discussions on feminine apparel is notoriously of absorbing interest to the male intelligence!

The thoroughbred girl will always show a neat foot. Few things are more deplorable than a smart-tailor-built outfit allied to old and shapeless shoes.

11. SIN AND SOCIETY

On a trip to Montreal in 1685, the French explorer Baron Louis de Lahontan noted in his journal that the local clergy was extremely repressive. "Here we cannot enjoy ourselves, either at play, or in visiting the ladies, but 'tis presently carried to the curate's ears, who takes notice of it in the pulpit. His zeal goes so far as to even name the persons." Two hundred years later, Kit was voicing a similar complaint. Canadian clergymen were right in preaching obedience to the Ten Commandants, she said, but they acted like petty dictators or narrow-minded asses when they warned congregations to avoid vaudeville houses, art exhibits, bicycling, or simply having too much fun in life. Toronto's Sunday-closure bylaw infuriated her. In 1834 a city ordinance banned all commercial activities on the Lord's Day except, for survival's sake, the sale of milk before 9 a.m. and after 4 p.m. Kit argued that as she was a God-loving Christian, she could not accept the theory that she would be corrupted, or the Lord would be offended, if she bought a bag of groceries upon leaving a Sunday service.

Her protests had little, if any, effect. Following the publication of an 1891 census revealing there were 61,127 pagans in Canada, the clergy felt all the more positive that the forces of evil were gaining ground across the land, and those opposing the Sabbath bylaw were part of the wicked onslaught. Methodist, Presbyterian and Roman Catholic thinking dominated the Dominion; hard work was exalted, fleshly pleasure condemned. Given the vast influence of the churches, Kit's comments on religious matters—sometimes irreverent, other times downright critical—were definitely not widely applauded.

The wild rush of female missionaries to the haunts of the heathen will not, one sincerely hopes, be encouraged by pastors and the heads of missionary societies. While it is acknowledged that women are the mainstays of the foreign missions, their religious fervor ought to be restrained in murderous times like these [shortly before the Boxer Rebellion broke out in 1900]. When women are bound to make heroines of themselves, they are apt to become hysterical. The calm, practical side of it is lost sight of when the gallant creatures rush into the breech. Somebody ought to prevent them. That there are more women in the world than men is no reason why the former must be massacred. Better that the heathen Chinese, bland and smiling, go to uttermost perdition than that one Christian woman be murdered.

Ralph: So you're boiling mad because the Salvation Army disturbs your Sunday rest with its drumming, singing and praying outside your window. Pay attention to what they're trying to tell you, Ralph, or the next quiet room you end up in may be in Hades.

Bible class meetings, choir practices, prayer meetings and working girls' associations are all right but set these against Yonge Street on a Saturday night, promiscuous flirtation, the theatre, etc., and which will win out? All the grave and reverend heads of girls' institutions seem to forget that the young things need a bit of excitement now and then, and they should provide pure and innocent pleasures in the way of an occasional gala night for their girls. Instead of denouncing theatres as ungodly, sinful places, why not treat their members to a night at Shea's music hall or the Princess Theatre? You know that if you boldly grasp a nettle it will not sting you, while if you toy with it, springing back when its innocent tooth bites in play, it will go in deeper and be awfully hard to pull out.

A Romantic Reader: I really cannot say how far religion interferes with a lady who is in love, not being in that tender predicament myself. Madame Severin, the famous *Punch* journalist, holds that no woman who is in love can at the same time thoroughly practice her religious duties. She may be right. To be pious is to think of God, and thinking of God is thinking of someone other than one's lover and, to be sure, a woman in love is incapable of thinking of anything beyond her love.

Not a word have I to say against those ladies who prefer to live in convents. Why shouldn't they if they have a mind to—although it must be a rather dull way of passing the time.

Lost Lamb: Do you think you ought to come to me? I fear I would make a bad shepherd, for it takes all my time to look after myself. Still, to answer you earnestly, this condition of self-distrust is a pitiful one to be in. It is destructive. When Peter began to doubt, he began to sink. You must not come to me with these questions in one breath: "Which is the true Church?", and, "Is it wrong to dance?" The first one I wisely let alone. To the second I reply, dancing is wrong when the minds of the dancers make it so. To those who tread the merry measure for its own sweet sake, it is a pure recreation.

There is an anecdote told in Rome about the Pope. His attendants, it seems, amass considerable wealth in the sale of his clothes. One day a high-bred French dame was admitted in audience, and threw herself at the feet of the Holy Father, expressing her gratitude at having regained her health through him. "How?" enquired the Pope. "I obtained possession of a sock that was worn by your Holiness," replied the lady, "and having put that amulet on my sick foot, I immediately recovered." "Madam," said the Pope, with an ironical smile, "you have indeed been fortunate. One of my socks has cured you, whilst I, who wear two pairs a day on each foot, can find no relief from my gout."

Very few women golf on Sundays. The reason most of them don't is not because of any religious scruples. It's because they believe in leaving the day free for the men. In all golf clubs there is an unwritten law, a tacit understanding, that upon the one day men are free to golf women should keep clear of the links. While the churches must be gratified at the paucity of

women on the Sabbath links, the fact that this is to encourage
men to play there—and not a case of admirable self-abstinence—
can be scarcely consoling.

Few things are funnier than typographical blunders, and an old
newspaperman who made a fad of collecting them has some
beauties in his scrapbook. The *Winnipeg Times,* on the death of
a reverend gentleman, meant to say "the death of a prelate" but
printed "the death of pirate" instead. The respected *Mail and
Empire* once said in Woman's Kingdom of a certain great actress
that "on the beast sparkled a diamond" instead of "on her
breast." A New York paper's report of a political meeting gave it,
"The snouts of 10,000 Democrats rent the air," when it was their
"shouts," not their noses. Ludicrous indeed—nay, awful—was
the blunder of a printer when he murdered a young reporter's account of Dr. Talmage's church service thus: "Dr. Talmage
wound up his service with the hymn, Nearer by God to Thee."
And another paper reporting a sermon had the same minister say
the next day his lady parishioners were "clothed scantily" when
he had said, "clothed with sanctity."

It is fifteen years since the Pope had been outside the walls of
the Vatican. What an exquisite prison it must be!

Personally, I think an atheist the most stupid of persons because
I do not find the non-existence of the Creator so much as think-
able. But like all other tribes, sects and groups atheists should
have full freedom of action and speech. We are fast learning that
prosecution or persecution for opinion must be either a blunder,
or a crime, or both. The movement towards tolerance is gaining
ground in the older countries. Culture will always bring it, and
perhaps the culminating point towards liberality was reached
when a Scottish professor of divinity, speaking in the most rigid
university in Britain, declared that the world owed a debt of
gratitude to the atheists who in the present century have fought
for freedom of opinion. Fifty years ago, he would have been
stoned and expelled from Scotland for that address.

A Sinner: So the preacher frightened you. Don't you realize that
the minute details of eternal punishment given by some ranters

are merely their own diseased imaginings? I remember once hearing an Englishman invent such a set of diabolical horrors that a woman in the church went raving mad. Such talks are libels on God, and are blasphemous to the last degree. Better not to go to church than to feel as you do now. Why, the shallowest observation of Nature teaches that beneficence, not maleficence, is God's rule. There is no such awfulness as that ignorant man describes. What would we do at the final moment if we had only thoughts of a vicious God? This life is hard enough as it is.

There is something really touching about the financial difficulties in which some of the big churches find themselves these days. The constant need that they have to pay expenses and interest on mortgages. And so the world of usury comes close to the house of God, and the money-changers have their stands almost within the doors. In boom times, when people made money hand over fist, it was not altogether a bad impulse that made them raise temples in thankfulness to the Power that in some dim way they connected with their luck. But the worst of it is the boom ebbed away, leaving the churches somewhat stranded, so that now piety has to take the shape of superhuman efforts to pay off the mortgages and to keep up to the demands of interest on the loans.

General Booth and the Salvation Army's much-criticized method of commending the Gospel to the masses may not be as refined a style of worship as the dean of the State church practices, but I have no doubt that it is quite acceptable to the Deity. After all, the established churches have no authority for supposing that the sonorous big drum is less pleasing to the Divine ear than the soft tone of the cathedral organ.

Too much religion can spoil domestic happiness. I know of a woman, a refined, wealthy lady, whose husband rarely comes near the grand mansion he calls his home. She has the sympathy of all, and he is called a villain. Years ago his wife got a taste for saving the souls of sinners, which generally means meddling with other people's affairs. She never thought about her husband's soul. She grew so spiritual that her husband was banished from her room because she wanted to say quiet prayers and to sing a hymn before she went to bed. The man soon got tired of it and, after a while, he got somebody less anxious about other people's souls and more interested in his personality. If ever an apostle was blessed, it was St. Paul for the good talkings he gave to womankind. Keep silent in churches, he said. Furthermore, there is no need to look for sinners outside while the sinners at home stand shivering before us. The woman who is a success in her own household is the one whose children will rise up and call her blessed.

Pater: What extraordinary names you have chosen for the babies. Satan and Michael! I should love to watch them growing and see if Satan outwits Michael—I put my money on the diabolical youngster. What did you say to the clergyman? Did you really find a man who would baptize Satan?

We are such a moral city and so logical in our conclusions as to what is and is not a sin. We shudder at the thought of Sunday street cars! Rich people may enjoy whatever mode of transportation they please on the sacred day, but the poor man must stay home because his nickel conveyance is taking a Sabbath rest. Carriages are for hire, boats are for hire, bicycles are for hire. But not street cars!

I am thinking about the "for ladies' only" lectures that have been given lately in this city by an "escaped nun." I confess I wonder at the numbers who went to these meetings, which were supposed to be too immoral for men to listen to. Where are our refined women? What good will it do women who are not Roman Catholics to hear these polluting things? A Catholic woman wouldn't go, and women of other persuasions don't need to be warned against "the crimes of the confessional." No, they merely went to gratify a low curiosity, a morbid love of revolting, indecent things, and, I suppose, when they came out, they looked upon every Roman Catholic woman they knew as an immoral, bad woman. Belonging to the Church of England, I cannot be accused of favoring Roman Catholics, but I thank God and my mother that I was at least taught as much refinement as will keep me from ever looking on at an execution, or attending a "for ladies' only" meeting.

Willie: So to you it looks "ridiculous" for me "to be sitting in that office scribbling away your time." I am making my living and my children's, friend, and am thankful for having scribbling to do. You are working too, are you not? In high places, no doubt, since you are a student of geology and astronomy. How nice it must be for you to feel superior. By the way, Willie, do you not think it odd that as the world expands in the eyes of men and they attain a knowledge that would have astonished their forbearers, there should grow up side by side with the world's progress in science, and the arts, a corresponding growth of our small selves —in other words, of egoism. Why should we think ourselves of such importance? I remember one Sunday when the ship I was on was lying off the island of Martinique, and the parson and I were leaning over the rail. "If this ship were to go down tonight, you would in all probability go down to Hell," he suddenly said. "And where would you go?" I asked. "Up to the Master I have served so long to enter into my reward." "To ask for your wages? But why should I be doomed to Hell?" "Because you did not attend service this morning!" His smug satisfaction at his own worthiness was something to astound one. We surely ought to combat this pitiful trick of self-conceit. Don't you agree with me, Sweet William?

Solomon was reckless when he said there was nothing new under the sun. Now we have clergyman charged with being intoxicated. He eluded the accusation by stating that he was a victim of weak ankles, which would not obey him on occasion. He did not make it clear whether it was this affliction or another that also induced him to read the First Lesson over twice in a row. Or if it was weak ankles that not only caused him to wobble, but also to have halting and incoherent speech. As the *Mail* poet hath it:

> Speak no more of influenza
> As the curse of modern days,

For we're threatened with a darker
Shadow of our devious ways.
When you rise to preach or lecture,
And you find that as you speak
Sentences will keep colliding,
Stop! Your ankles must be weak.

12. FADS AND FETISHES

Rebecca Lang was no ordinary teacup reader. Charging double the normal fee, she made the rounds of Toronto's affluent districts, giving private readings. Upon learning of her reputedly superior talents, Kit put aside enough money to have Rebecca call every Tuesday afternoon at the boardinghouse where she lived before she remarried. Rebecca, a charismatic, white-haired lady, carried her own cups from house to house, claiming they had special powers. Seated at a small table in Kit's room, she studied the leaves with the concentration of a spellbound mystic: it was not unusual for five minutes to pass without her saying a word. Kit often scoffed at fortunetellers and mystics but, the truth was, she was susceptible to the more convincing practitioners of the ancient crafts. When Rebecca cautioned her against going on a June vacation, Kit went in August. And Rebecca's instructing her to be kinder to the underprivileged prompted Kit to hand a street-corner beggar a fistful of coins. The relationship between Kit and the teacup seer ended when a friend of Kit's happened to mention that Rebecca had been at her house the day after her session with Kit. Rebecca had given identical readings: both women were informed that brown was their lucky color and that a young, handsome acquaintance was secretly in love with them. The following Tuesday, Kit dismissed the teacup specialist at the front door. "You are repeating yourself," she snapped. "Don't you wash the cups between readings?" The experience soured Kit permanently on teacup readers but she remained interested in unusual practices, whether they were the strange rites of African natives or the tribal customs of the supposedly more enlightened Anglo-Saxons.

Can thirteen really be an unlucky number? Then, Uncle Sam should look at his quarter dollars. On each are thirteen stars, thirteen letters in the scroll the eagle holds in his claws, thirteen feathers in the Great Baldheaded's tail, thirteen lines on the shield, thirteen arrowheads, and there are thirteen letters in the world quarter-dollar. But you and I wouldn't mind a gift of a million of those same "unlucky" quarter dollars, would we?

In South Africa the savage tribes have a ceremony which they put the matrimonial candidate through previous to his entering the holy state. His hands are tied in a bag full of fire ants for two hours. If he bears, unmoved, the torture of their stings, he is considered qualified to cope with the daily nagging, the jar and the fret of married life. Such a man would make an ideal husband. He would not be upset by the new spring bonnet or an overdone steak. However, they do say there are a good many oldmaids out in those parts.

The Queen has a horror of peacocks' feathers. She is possessed of an idea that should she ever look upon those feathers, misfortune will follow within a few hours. In the Royal collection of plate at Windsor, there is a magnificent jewelled peacock worth fabulous sums. This piece the Queen will never allow to be placed on the table at any of the great functions but, as a sort of compromise, it always graces the centre of the giant sideboard behind Her Majesty's chair, and she never turns her eyes that way.

Reading about the attack by the French and the British on the cannibals of the Pacific Islands brings to mind a horrible tribe in India, who haunt the burning grounds with the purpose of snatching and eating the flesh of the dead if refused the alms they demand. Curiously enough, this horrible race are called Aghori, which is supposed to be the original form of the word "ogre," usually derived from Orcus, the ruler of the internal regions.

Three boys were playing near one of the temples of Nassick recently when a hungry Aghori pounced on one of them and proceeded to eat him while he was still living. In Kathiawar and in northern India, especially about Benares, two thousand Aghoris still live and for this reason the authorities do not approve of Europeans going unattended into the hills. Perhaps the most curious thing about these appalling people is that they clothe their wickedness in philosophy. They claim that the true principle of existence is to be indifferent to all that is, and to treat one substance the same as another.

One sees in their awful teachings a reaction against the laws of caste, which cuts them off from their fellow-men. One might draw a parallel between them and the anarchists. An anarchist who preaches the doctrine of anarchy and dies for it is the misbegotten child of over-weening despotism; so surely the Aghori may be the outcome of those stringent caste rules which shut him off from fellowship of his kind and, greatly oppressed, he practices his grim doctrine. One shudders at such deductions.

There are still many who believe in the infallibility of the charm. Not the uneducated only carry about on their persons little bits of superstition to offset any bad luck that may be coming their way. Grave and respected citizens have been known to carry a potato in their pockets as a preventive of pain in their bones. Why should a potato be selected as the irresistible foe of bone-ache? Because Saint Patrick was afflicted with a pain in his elbow and potatoes being the only thing cheap and plentiful in Ireland, he picked one up in a field, blessed it and put it in his missal-bag.

Some people say that if you eat boiled nettles three times during the month of March you will escape fever for a year. Many is the unsavory mouthful we took in our youthful days—days which were also devoted to draughts of wormwood mixtures, sulphur, brimstone and other blood-clearing delicacies.

I have known old ladies to carry such things in their weird pockets as a horse's tooth (against cramps), a double hazelnut (against toothache), and the bone of a goose (against all ill-luck). Not so long ago, at a gathering of twenty lawyers, ministers and other professional men, the talk turned to carrying a horse chestnut as a preventative of rheumatism, and no less than thirteen confessed that they had chestnuts in their pockets at that very minute. A lady once tried to cure herself of ague by putting a caterpillar in a box and carrying it about with her.

A crooked sixpence brings luck but you must carry it in your left-side pocket. Even the burglar has his charm, a piece of coal. To dream of coal signifies riches, probably that is why the burglar chooses it as his amulet. The bank robber is never caught who travels with the paw cut off from a live mole somewhere on his person.

A bit of broken pipeshank preserves its wearers from cancer while the tip of a mouse's tail, cut from the creature while alive, is a sure preventative of consumption. Not so easy to get is the heart of a turtle, a cure for jaundice, while a frog's liver will keep you forever outside an asylum. Of watch-chain charms—a half moon will hold love forever. A seal is not a lucky thing for a boy to give a girl but vice-versa is sure to bring luck. A cross should never be worn by a man; it is lucky for women. A charm in the shape of a musical instrument brings fame to its wearer; a silver moon brings health, and a snake brings long life.

Delightful is the simplicity of charm-keeping. There must be much childishness left in the world after all, and it is very good leaven.

A social fad this winter is ghosts. A number of girls gather together for the evening, and turn down the lights, and huddle on sofas, while someone draws dreadful squeakings from a violin. Then somebody else stands on the hearthrug and talks ghosts, and vampires, and dead hands, and all sorts of gruesome things that make them jump when a withered twig knocks on the window. That's all. When everyone is comfortably frightened, they light up and eat sandwiches.

Beware of the woman who has too much white in her eyes. The woman whose eyes slant towards the nose is a man's woman. (After five minutes' steady staring into my toilet-glass, I have arrived at the conclusion that I am not a man's woman.) The woman whose eyes are too close together is apt to prove treacherous and insincere. The woman whose eyes are far apart is a close observer and is generally friendly to the opposite sex, and generous to her own. The clear grey eye belongs to the business woman and the blue eye to women of all kinds.

What about men's eyes? The grey-eyed man is cautious and observing. He has a level head so it won't do to play tricks on him. He is not easily coaxed and if those grey eyes droop at the corners, steer clear of him. The droops may give him a pathetic look but he will have a temper, and be a bit deceitful and sensual. The brown-eyed man is always hopeful and generous—a cheery, lovable fellow. I shouldn't mind having a brother with brown eyes. Nor a husband either.

How is it that we have people moving Heaven and earth to put a stop to the liquor traffic and the use of opium and not one to suggest a reform in the sleeping draught traffic that goes on in the nursery? A letter to Woman's Kingdom coolly advises the use of opiates in the nursery and begs me to write an article on the subject, recommending it as "a valuable practice for worn-out women, who otherwise might be kept wakeful all night by a fretful child."

Heaven forbid that any such doctrine should be found in these columns. On the contrary, it cannot be too vigorously denounced. If it be right to drug a peevish infant to sleep, why is there all this commotion over adults who, by their own will, seek the same end with drink or the opium pipe? Of the two, baby-drugging is by far the worst for the tiny creatures have no choice. The effect of chloral, laudanum, or other sleep-producing drugs on children is disastrous, a toss up between an early death or a sickly life. Better to let the baby howl at night, or even to spank it!

Tibble: "How is a woman silently accredited as past her first youth in society?" When she is offered a Scotch and soda at the end of the evening: the "others," not necessarily younger, but accepted as such, being regaled on soft drinks.

Of all fads perhaps the most fascinating is that of collecting. Coins, stamps, old china, silver or copper. Fans, gems, antique furniture—all or anything so long as you are a collector. It is the fashion to be a monomaniac and collecting is the correct mania. Some collect for the intrinsic value of the articles collected, some for sheer pleasure of possession, others for the vulgar reason that other people, fashionable people, collect things and they must follow the bell-wether.

I know a man who will sit by the hour over his case of birds' eggs, now and again handling some fragile specimen with tender care while he relates its history. Every egg in that cabinet has its own story, and the man grows a boy again as he tells tales of hairbreadth escapes and tall climbings.

China collecting has gone out. It was a brisk fad while it lasted and its relics remain in many a dim cabinet and polished top shelf. China will come in again and rare bits of blue Hawthorn and square-mark Worcester will go on parade again.

Coin collectors are to have an inning; so are collectors of miniatures, fans, snuff-boxes and lace. The Princess of Wales has the finest collection of fans in the world. Exquisite things of chicken skin with laid-down mounts finished with Verius Martin (nothing more than a marvellous secret varnish invented by the coach-builder Martin, to whom society ladies of his time sent their fans); fans with sombre tortoise shell pique sticks, and fans delicately painted by long-deceased French artists.

Queen Victoria was a collector of relics of the early Stuarts. She once paid £160 for Prince Charles Edward's walking stick. Queen Helena of Italy goes in for boots and shoes. Insects worth ten thousand pounds live at Tring, a Rothschild estate, in thirty insect cabinets. Silver pins are used to keep these rich bugs in place and a staff of curators look after them. The Lonsdale family have an extremely fine collection of whips, Patti runs to daggers, Ellen Terry to pinces-nez, while Bernhardt wanders in fancy from barbaric gems to human bones.

In medical circles, some queer collections have been made. Dr. Lugs of the Salpetriere's dainty fad was composed of twenty-two hundred brains and Dr. Burt Wilder of Cornell University is credited with a similar collection and also with having persuaded friends to swell his store by bequeathing to him the contents of their skulls.

Menu cards are a favorite fad with many collectors, as are theatre programmes. The Isarina has a series of programmes bound in red morocco while pictorial post-cards are the very latest craze. The Prince of Wales is an ardent collector of these. A collector, whose collecting turned to a mania for hat crowns, once collected no less than one hundred thousand of these. He had to steal most of them. He used to frequent theatre dressing rooms, concert halls and even dark passages and entranceways of private houses in order to swell his collection.

Drink makes gentle men cruel; well-balanced men brutish; polished men cads; intellectual men saddened imbeciles; honest men thieves. It makes all things foul that should be of good report.

The Chinese who pursue the art of palmistry do not confine their investigation to the palm only: they examine the nails too. Tapering nails mean brains; hard and thick nails, old age; coarse, stumpy nails, dullness of wit; bright yellow nails, high rank to come; dark, thin nails, obscurity; fresh white nails, love of ease; half-moon-shaped nails, health and happiness; sharply-tipped nail, cleverness; really rough nails, stupidly; nails like the end of a plank, staunch sincerity. The Chinese push every investigation of this kind to its logical conclusion. Consequently, when they have exhausted palmistry, they proceed to 'solistry,' and extract indications from the lines of the feet.

There is always some new fad, and just now it is having your vibrations read. You simply sit back and let the "medium" take your aura and read your soul-waves. It goes like this: "I see a purple aura emanating from you." You look about you trying to see it too. "Now it changes to green. You are cynical about something. Don't be cynical." The "medium" sees strange rays of all colors. She implores you to be sunny, to go to bed early, to get up with the lark. "Your vibrations are off-color. Work. Do something worthwhile. Your aura tells me you're an idler." "Madam," you stutter, rising to get out. "I am a worker. I work all the time." "Oh, no," she says. "An aura cannot lie." Wordless, you totter out with your green aura and your purple soul-waves and making for the nearest tea-room, proceed to turn your aura a deep, dark brown.

Hearten to the lover's litany, as compiled by the ancients. To ensure good luck, you will, if you are engaged in: January, Exchange locks of hair with your sweetheart; February, Exchange silver motto rings; March, He gives her his right-hand glove, while she offers him her left-hand sheath; April, Exchange neck ties; May, Eat three daisies each in one another's presence; June, Each lover to write an ode to matrimony and to exchange same; July, His bootlace for her shoe-string; August, His handkerchief for her garter; September, He offers the lady a hazelnut, she re- sponds with a peanut; October, He gives her three hazelnuts, she responds with a nut-cracker; November, Break an apple and eat half in each other's presence; December, Pluck each an eyelash fom the nether lid, and exchange them.

Let me tell you about the singularly fat lady who was staying at Ascot for the race week. On the first morning of her visit, the maid filled her hip bath but when the lady sat down in it the water ran over and there was a vacuum. The lady tugged and pulled but failed to extricate herself from the bath so, with this shell on her back, she crawled like a turtle across the floor, steer- ing for the bell. The maid answered the bell, pulled the bath and pulled the lady, but there was no separating them. So, they wrapped the fat dame in a blanket and called the village black- smith who punched a hole in the bath, let in the air and let out the lady.

Football to the woman who for the first time sees the game is an astonishing jumble of strong men racing about a field and punching one another with unnecessary vim. There seems nei- ther beginning nor end to it; but as you watch the fellows tum- bling over each other on the grass, and hear the ringing shouts from the grandstand, a touch of excitement creeps into you, and you rap your umbrella on the bench and, with effort, refrain from shrill encouragement.

What effect will smoking cigarettes have on a woman? It will blacken her teeth, befoul her breath, disgust her friends and repel her admirers. Many girls think it is a fine and spirited thing to smoke cigarettes before men. They think it attracts them, that it is pretty and chic. As a matter of fact, nine out of ten men are disgusted by such conduct, while the small remainder, though they may be amused by the unfeminine performance, would, when their laughter is done, despise the woman. They might say with a smile that she is "good fun" and "awfully jolly," but they would never dream of respecting her, hardly of loving her, and not at all of marrying her.

A brisk and tart lady writes me a brisk and tart letter upon the temperance question. From what I can gather from her garbled production, I am accused of upholding in this column drunkenness and the lawlessness therein. To say that I am astounded by the accusation is to say little. People fail to discriminate between temperance and outright prohibition. The writer of this letter asks that I advise young girls to boycott socially not only drunkards but "all young men who are not total abstainers." I'm afraid the girls would have to dance with one another for lack of a fitter partner if such a boycott was declared.

Here are some old superstitions about death. The shooting forth of a roll of tallow from the top of a lighted candle is called a winding sheet, and gives warning of an approaching death in the house. A cinder bounding from the fire is either a purse or a coffin, the will-o'-wisp indicates, if small and pale blue, the death of a child; if large and yellow, the death of a matured age. If crickets suddenly leave a house that they have long inhabited, it is a sign of death. The tapping made by a small beetle called the death-watch is said to be a warning of death; so is the howling of a dog at night. This is all very silly chatter; if any of it were true, I would have been playing a saintly harp long ago.

In the old days, the scandalmonger used to have to sit in the stocks, and it is a shame they don't revive the custom now. Women say the most terrible things about women without flinching. It is none of your business, and it's none of mine, where a woman gets her clothes. It is none of your business, and it's none of mine, as to the relations between people, so long as they behave properly in public places. My friend, we kneel beside sinners in churches and we are going to meet them in many other places. The scandalmonger elects herself a saint. Yet I never hear a woman talking about another woman, announcing that she knows they are fast women, or that she knows they are drunkards, that I don't feel like asking if she hasn't gone among just such a set to have gained all this information. Good women don't know: it is only women who have gone through the mill who can carefully pick out the chaff from the wheat.

13. THE ARTS

"*My God, we are like sisters!*" *With that exuberant cry, Sarah Bernhardt grabbed Kit's hand and led her from the dressing-room door to a table mirror. As they studied their reflections in the oval glass, both acknowledged there was a distinct facial resemblance. Whatever similarity existed between Kit and the Divine Sarah was limited to their physical appearance and, of course, a common dedication to their respective crafts. For Kit's eccentricities were mild in comparison to those of the actress known as the Eighth Wonder of the World. Sarah slept in a padded coffin, used a pet python for a footstool, hunted alligators, and occupied front-row seats for four executions, including a garroting and two beheadings. During her maiden North American tour in 1880, the French star enhanced her bizarre reputation by running out onto a St. Lawrence River ice floe, going down in a Pennsylvania coal mine, and firing a cannon at an Illinois munitions factory. As for her moral conduct, the Archbishop of Montreal likened her to the Whore of Babylon and advised Quebec Catholics to boycott her performances, an admonition that, naturally, resulted in packed houses. Returning to Montreal to appear at the Academy of Music theater in 1898, Sarah said Canada was a culturally deprived, semibarbarous place. Kit did not mention the actress's well-publicized statement, or her moral attitudes, in the revealing story she wrote about her. She was so captivated by Sarah's acting that she could not bring herself to censure her, as other journalists did. Plainly, Kit did not agree that Canada was a cultural outback. She knew no Canadian city rivaled Paris, London, and New York, but she maintained that the arts were on the threshold of a fabulous boom: all that was needed was persistent attention and a proper mixture of encouragement and valid criticism. Doing her bit to help the flowering process, Kit wrote extensively about the stage, literature, art, and classical music.*

An artist, giving a concert, should not demand an entrance fee but should ask the public to pay just before leaving, as much as they like. From the sum he would be able to judge what the world thinks of him—and we would have fewer mediocre concerts.

Bernhardt took me with her to the Academy of Music and sat me in a corner where I would be out of the way while she dressed. She put on a black gown of lace—a loose wrapper it seemed rather than a dress. It hung about her in a cloud, and one wondered how she would ever get it into shape. She took some turquoise gems from her case and set them—great blue stars!—here and there in the dark lace. One at the hem, one at the side, one on the shoulder; anywhere and everywhere. They held the dress in place and the woman looked as though the stars had fallen and clung there.

She carefully arranged her hair, heaping it about her long eyes, every twist and tendril for effect. Then she drew dark violet lines about her eyes that elongated and narrowed them, touched her ears with rouge, her lips, her cheeks, slightly, very slightly. And then she bolted the door for a moment, and taking a little phial, poured from it a drop into each eye, closing them quickly as if in pain. It was belladonna. Afterwards, I noticed the magnificent effect of the blinding fluid. The pupils large, black, were dilated to their fullest extent. The eye itself was languorously beautiful.

She walked to the stage amid a silence. We were all grouped behind the scenes, and through a crack in them, I watched her. It was the scene where Fedora betrays her lover to his enemies. I saw this woman who had been so particular as to her appearance but a moment before change in an awful way as the reality of her role forced itself upon her. The first change was in the hands. They crooked slowly at her sides, and in a flash were raised to her hair, stirring there frantically. She pulled the thick red mass of it up from her forehead, revealing it fully, her plainest feature. The face grew gaunt, haggard, old. Every line showed. She grew pallid, drawn. It was an old woman who faced the people—with the mark of all passions on that terrible face; the eyes burned with a dark magnificence; the exquisite child-voice stirred oddnesses in the heart.

When the curtain fell, she walked slowly by, straight to her dressing room, and fell into a chair there. I dared not speak. She let me kiss her hand, which was enough for me then. The maid drew off her shoes, her silk stockings. Then Madame stood up and we saw the great rent in the bosom of her lace gown where she had clutched it. "A night's work for me," said the maid in a whisper. Presently Bernhardt spoke. "Ces les emotions, les emotions que me tourmente," she said slowly, still pallid and large-eyed.

Then came the thunder of the Marseillaise from the crowd. In a second the greatest actress the world has ever known leaped towards the door, clapping her hands. "Vive la France, la belle France!" she cried. Her face flushed like that of a girl. All youth glorified her in that moment. One shrank into one's corner, a small, ignorant, insignificant creature. Why did God give such gifts to the one woman, denying the other, one murmured feebly. Ah, heaven, what a tragedy, an intellectual tragedy, it is to fall short, to feel that God began once to kindle the fire of genius in a human soul, but let it go out for want of a divine bellows.

Why can't we have better plays in Toronto? For the past two seasons we have been no better off than the merest village. Burlesques, spectacular absurdities we have had in plenty, but plays —good plays and good actors—have been rare as oases in the Sahara. A week ago there was Antony and Cleopatra, depending on scenery and one woman's beauty. McDowell's sibilant noises did not become a Mark Antony, and Miss Walsh, radiant, exquisite of form, young, was lacking in subtle grace. Then a Caesar with a Scotch accent—by the gods!

Lovers of the Brownings will possibly be glad to hear that the love-letters of the two splendid poets are to be published. Before his death, Browning destroyed all his papers, with the exception of the letters that passed between him and Elizabeth Barrett. These were carefully preserved; they were tied-up in tiny

packets, each envelope being numbered, and kept in an inlaid
box, into which the letters fitted exactly. While still in vigorous
health, Browning used these words concerning them: "There
they are; do with them as you please when I am gone."

It seems to me that such intimate correspondence as love-letters is too sacred to be given to the wide world. There is too
much diving into the lives of those who make great books. Since,
however, Mr. Browning showed no objection to having his love-
words made public, why should we? Still, one wonders what
gentle Elizabeth Barrett would say if she could speak from
choirs invisible.

Isn't it strange that art is the only serious pursuit on earth and
yet the artist is the only person who is never serious?

The Jersey Lily [the English actress Lillie Langtry] was sitting, a
radiant figure, in the little old greenroom fitted up for the time as
the "star" dressing room. It was between the second and third
acts of The Degenerates [in Toronto, 1900], and Mrs. Langtry
wore a blue satin gown, starred with brilliants, and sweeping in
heavy folds to the door of the small room. About her throat lay a
necklace of big turquoises and diamonds, and a long chain of
gems, ending in a large pearl. Rays of light seemed to radiate
from the gems that flashed on neck and bosom. All about lay rich
gowns and cloaks, satin shoes, jewels, laces, trinkets in abun-
dance, while the table was heaped with the paraphernalia of
stage make-up.

There is an air of simplicity about the famous English beauty
that is very attractive. Her manner, her speech, her gestures all
speak of one who has been used to moving in what are termed
the highest social circles. Many actresses not quite as famous or
as beautiful will receive a newspaperwoman with an air of con-
descension, with a brusqueness of manner, or with a silly affecta-
tion. Mrs. Langtry indulges in none of these mannerisms. She is
simple, direct, helpful and dignified.

Mrs. Langtry has had much abuse heaped upon her. Some of
the milder epithets used in her regard have described her as
hard, cold, unsympathetic. A moment's quiet observation and
conversation with her proves absolutely the falsity of this judg-

ment. There is a great deal of womanliness and kindness about Mrs. Langtry, and these, added to her beauty, make her a most appealing personality.

We talked of the pro-Boer proclivities of our friends across the border.

"My tour has been a financial success," she said, "in spite of the opposition of a few Americans. I say a few advisedly because it would be unfair to the great mass of people across the line, who have always given me a brilliant reception, not to discriminate. Of course, I was misled by the sympathetic attitude of the British people and press towards the United States into thinking the latter would warmly espouse the cause of the Empire in our war with the Boers. It was not as an actress, or because of my harmless little play, that I have been abused by the yellow journals. It was because I am an English woman.

"As it was, however, only two American cities refused to permit the play to be staged, Detroit and Philadelphia. We met with a cordial welcome in Boston, New York, everywhere else. Still, I was glad when I felt under the old flag again. I knew no one would insult me in Canada."

"These things do hurt, I suppose?"

"They do," said Mrs. Langtry, after some hesitation. "But the only way is not to look for them, think about them, or read about them. Besides, it is only the lower class of journal that would print insults. I avoid those altogether."

Shelley's poetry is exquisite but I would not like to people the earth with men of his sort. He was a reckless and undutiful son; he married a woman who was in no way suited to become his wife; and then he deserted her and she committed suicide. Why condone the brutality—for he insulted his wife grossly—because he had genius? The man was immoral. A genius, but touched with the slime of animalism.

Unclassical: You certainly can be a lover of music without adoring the absolutely classical. A man may prefer a gavotte by Gluck to an aria by Sir Arthur Sullivan but, too, he may prefer the latter. Because you cannot understand the pain and passion and triumph of the Eroica is no reason why you cannot take delight in Home, Sweet Home. Don't be downcast about it. Be sure that the people who tell you they can't find any melody in Ye Banks and Braes, and who affect to slobber over Wagner, know as little what real music means, whether interpreted by a Scottish bard or a German maestro, as they do of the personnel of the inhabitants of Mars.

Ibsen is a much safer topic than George Bernard Shaw. That individual is best kept for a boudoir or smoking room topic.

A Winnipeg bookseller spends thousands of dollars every year in advertising his name and address with just this simple admonition, "Empty your purse into your head." He should have added, "and hear it rattle," for the books he sells are utter trash.

The highly-fed lawyer is often a poet or novelist killed. There are shocking tragedies in life.

A dreadful book comes to me for review. I will not name it for to do so would be to advertise it. The book is one that a bad man might put in the hands of a certain type of girl, assured that its reading would bring her, a willing victim, to his arms. Oh, women friends, why is it that we women put the mightiest weapons against our sex into the hands of men? The average woman-novel of today is a dissolute, hideous, sensual, coarse horror, telling, as too often sensational journals tell, how best to commit an outrage, an indecency, beside which murder is tame. Next to some of the novels that are every day advertised on the show-boards of the booksellers Zola is a purist. And too many of these books are by women authors.

Eleonora Duse is not beautiful. [Kit observed the renowned Italian actress in Montreal in 1897.] That is, as beauty is usually counted, but her mere physical being is charged with what we call attractiveness and fascination. She has a magnetic personality, but it is without the seductiveness of a Bernhardt. The Italian actress gives the impression that a door locked and sealed gives. You read nothing of the real story in that lean form, that melancholy face, that gentle, queenly bearing. Glitterings you have, hints of much suffering borne nobly, of a past that has been intensely sad, but which has left no bitterness, no hardness of the soul.

Much of this woman's attractiveness lies in the strangely-wearied look with which she looks at you out of her big eyes. Not that I would have you think that she appears wearied by the hard work or the prostration that follows the portrayal of great passions on the stage. Rather it is a soul-weariness, full of gentleness and pity, as though the woman was always looking for sympathy and not finding any.

An immense femininity pervades all Duse's acting. When she portrays the woman in love she gives you the woman who leans on the man, who looks to him for protection, who appeals to his manliness, his courage, all there is in him of chivalry. Whether she plays Fedora or Camille, La Tosca or Frou-frou, she approaches her lover with the caressing, tender, timid attitude of an adoring woman. Her utter loneliness, as seen in her acting—that wearied child-like smile, that wistful face, no longer young, that spare form—sadden, oppress and allure you. Forever Duse will remain in your memory as the incarnation of sensitive femininity.

Everybody likes new books. Nicely gotten-up books with every dainty luxury of binding, soft paper and gorgeous printing. How a book collector purrs and strokes a rare edition; he shows you the cover, he rejoices in the feel of the paper. But think of the tattered editions out of which we have sucked sweetness and honey in days gone by. I mind of a library I kept in a potato-cellar in our garden at home. On the rim of the potato shelves were set cabbages whose broad leaves sheltered my Dickens, Thackeray and Ouida, my Gulliver's Travels, Crusoe and Pilgrim's Progress. Down in the cellar a wild red-haired girl lay reading between bites of an apple. Ah, how lovely. How I wish I could clasp again with the same vim of delight even one of those thumbed, dog-eared volumes that lay in the potato-cellar. Little Colleen of ages past, if only you were here to fill with your buoyant hope and gladness of life the tired heart of a woman. Little Kathleen, so long dead and buried, amid the bogs of the homeland.

The literary part of the *Canadian Magazine* is almost as interesting as its numerous pages of advertising which, as magazines go, is saying a good deal.

A French doctor has been finding out about Emil Zola, and the result of his study is that the instinct for self-preservation is a prominent trait in the author. He is not afraid of the bicycle but when the train he is travelling on enters a tunnel Zola is beset with the idea that the two ends will fall in and bury him alive. He shrinks from riding through a forest at night, and in his house he counts the steps of his staircases and the different things in his bureau over and over again. He must touch the same pieces of furniture a certain number of times before he goes to sleep, and there are numbers that he feels have a good or bad influence on him. As, for instance, the number seven. Seven times a night he opens and shuts his eyes before he settles to sleep. Seven times he touches his watch, his lamp, his book. And yet he is not at all insane. He has ragged moments, all right, but so have we, but we do not have his clearness of judgment, power of concentration, tenacity of effort, nor, alas, do we have his fame and money.

Ireland and Russia are sisters in many ways. Tourguenieff and Tolstoi always remind me of Ireland. The same pathos, savagery, gloom; the same spirit of rebellion, treachery, suspicion; the same atmosphere of the spiritual, the unseen; and the same love of revenge, barbaric modesty, and ghastly flippancy.

I heard Paderewski the other day. If it could be that such a wonderful musician could improve, the Pole has arrived at it. No wonder the women went mad, though in my soul I believe the craziness was more over his hair—that extraordinary reddish shock—and his thin, artistic face than over his playing. It was the matinee, and nearly all women. They ate marrons glacé while they waited, and between crunches one could hear: "Dear, Payderyewski, he is as long-haired as ever. I love Payderyewski so. I come to every performance."

"Paddywhiski is the most delightful performer on the pi-anno I ever heard play," said an Irish lady of distinguished accent to her friend while she withered under a glance from the woman who had called him Payderyewski.

"Delicious Padewrooski!" "Divine Pawderwschyyptsky. Why can't people pronounce his name properly?"

"Wonderfully gifted man, that Pahderwheffschkyi. Do you notice how few people give the Polish accent to his name."

"Some people think they know everything," said a pert American girl between crunches of chocolates. "The man's name is Paddwheweffswitchski. Why can't they say it right?"

Long-haired, or short-haired, rooski or wheffsky, it didn't matter once he came on [in Toronto, 1895]. As he broke into Schumann's minor sonata, you looked attentively at this frail creature who was exhibiting a power that was almost demonical. You saw a thin spiritual face surrounded by unkempt hair and full of expression more like pain than anything else.

The slender figure is very quiet. No swaying, no air-clawing, no pounding. The young Pole is above all things reverent in his attitude towards music. It is as if he saw the goddess and knows her moods. His touch is firm as steel but smooth as velvet; his intensity, his virility and delicacy strike one with amazement. At once, poetic fervor, dignity and caressing softness. At once, storm and passion, the "der grosse zug," and the exquisite singing tone.

Paderewski is without a doubt the greatest performer on the piano in the world. If you have heard him before, you will know him so vast in his improvement. He is absolutely perfect.

Literature would pay better if there were not so many dead men still in the business, hogging the customers.

It is odd but women writers, as a rule, make their heroes brutes. The insolent, cruel man is generally the person round whom they build their stories. Charlotte Brontë, Ouida, Corelli—they have all at one time or another idealized brutal men. The rule is too universal to be merely accidental. The Sabine women admired their Romans: the cruel and masterful in man must appeal to some instinct in the female gender.

The funniest mistake I ever saw was the way Da Vinci's name was written upon the brow of the Chicago Art Institute—Leonardo D. A. Vinci.

What is the matter with Canadian literature? Toronto is called the Boston of Canada, the Athens of the Dominion. And yet we are barely keeping up on our own publications. There are good writers in Canada. Do we help them? Why is it always the same about a prophet in his own country? Why do our writers have to leave us to make fame in other lands? People laugh at Canadian literature. I know for a fact that books bearing Canadian names or treating Canadian subjects are damned by publishing firms. It is all our own fault. And it is not as if we are a nation of fools. Or are we?

There is a threat that some publisher is going to print George Sand's letters to Chopin. Let us hope it will never be fulfilled. The Pagello revelations are more than enough. George Sand was a strong woman who ought to have been a man. She was morally a two-sexed being, a sort of moral hermaphrodite. In affairs of love she was the aggressor. She demanded of men that they love her, and they generally acceded to the demand. But she was great, and she had more than a touch of tenderness.

That Pagello, after all these years, should bring to light in the columns of the newspapers accounts of their relations and the marvellous love-letters George Sand wrote to him is one of the saddest showings of poor humanity. George Sand was the first Decadent. She was the founder of that school of yellow journalism which has given us novels of the Jude the Obscure type. No other woman, except perhaps Catherine of Russia, can mate with her. A mixture of poetic idealization and sensual attractions, given to wild outbursts of love and jealousy.

Yet with all this, the most industrious of women, one who after six or eight hours of writing could sit down and knit stockings; one who in church, kneeling before Him who welcomes everybody, and pardons everybody, would cover her face and weep bitterly in a fit of sensible devotion over shortcomings that she insisted that she could not help committing.

She had it in her to be a model wife and mother—affectionate, charitable, industrious. What feeling should the memory of such a woman inspire? Disgust? Admiration? Neither; but a mournful sense of regret that the divine and the base, the highest exaltation of the spirit and the most brutal demands of the flesh, often fight within the narrow bounds of the soul. Hyde and Jekyll fought for supremacy in the soul of George Sand. Who shall say that at the last supreme moment the good spirit was not the ascendant?

This is the day of the reciter. Their voices are loud throughout the land. And very pleasant entertainments recitations can be. It is delightful to think of the Ruskin family, with their intense seriousness, their reticence, their fastidious taste. The elder Ruskin read the whole of Pope and most of Dryden and Shakespeare to his wife and boy. And what family today is there that has not had its readings aloud from Thackeray and Dickens? Ah, those quiet family readings that have given away to the modern dramatic reciter who struts a mimic stage and, I'm afraid, so often rants. This being has invaded our living rooms. Not so long ago, in fact, I saw a young woman on my hearthrug making what seemed like frantic efforts to pull her hair out.

And who has not met the young man incurably afflicted with the desire to recite on any and all occasions? He makes the blood of the bravest turn cold. He comes in at all hours, and stamps up and down on the floor, reciting Eugene Aram's Dream. He is a little man, with creaky boots. A good reciter is well worth going to hear, but a sort of plague has broken out and every callow youth and school-room miss these days is reciting and their outpourings are sometimes difficult to bear. To hear Henry Irving, as happily I once had the pleasure, recite Eugene Aram is a revelation; not a few hold that his rendering of the poem is the only perfect performance he has given. His mannerisms help to emphasize the stark horror of the verses, and the effect is weird beyond description.

Up-to-date drawing-room recitations often have something about a dying child, or a deserted husband, or a flower girl, or a long-winded tramp, a shipwreck or a railroad accident. The boy still stands on the burning deck too. But a new style has gained ground. The sentimental Bret Harte-cum-Dickens "poem" is rather the rage now, and the favorite motive for the "poem" is the sudden discovery of exalted virtue in the lowest of the low, the roughest of the rough. Dukes and fair dames and bold outlaws have had their day, while the mewling newsboy, or tough navvy with a heart of gold, or a decayed, dying washer woman holds the floor. And these farragoes of doggerel are called "celebrated poems." Heaven defend us from the man who perpetrates them, and even more so from the people who recite them.

14. MORE HEARTS TO MEND

Kit's home address was a tightly kept secret. The lovelorn section had many regular correspondents who took her advice so seriously that they pleaded with the newspaper staff to let them speak to her personally about their latest crisis. The distressed lovers were almost beyond themselves whenever Kit fell ill and did not turn in a column. Get-well gifts of flowers, chocolates, wine, lace hankies, fruit, and books of poetry blitzed the editorial office; home remedies and bottles of patent medicine also arrived and, on one occasion, a thoughtful young man delivered a package of cheese in case Kit was too sick to shop for Patsy Brannigan. Kit made it a rule not to meet any of the correspondents face to face, but she broke the rule if she feared anyone was distraught enough to take their own life.

An Observer: You make rather sweeping assertions. A pretty face does not necessarily imply "no brains." The old idea that clever girls are dowdy, plain and untidy must surely be exploded by now. Have you travelled much?

Misery, Uncomfortable: You were a very foolish woman to have had a fit of crying over so small a thing. I have often been left hanging on my strap in the street car while gentlemen have got up and made room for nice-looking young girls. One has not forgotten the time when such little attentions were paid to oneself. They will be paid again, you know, when one's hair is white and one's back bent. My dear, have sense. Youth and beauty will always get the best things and you and I and the rest of us ought to be glad of the humble crumbs.

Anxious Bessie: Do you expect Fortune to knock at your door and, entering, to fill your lap with gold? God helps those who help themselves, my woman. Get up and work. Only the lilies of the field can exist and look pretty without toiling.

R.M.: Good gracious! Do you expect an angel for your wife? And what sort of man are you to write to a newspaper like this. So she is bright and vivacious—"much too lively"—and this is her great crime. Look backward for a moment and you will find that was her great charm when you were courting her. You must be a very disagreeable man to live with.

J.K.: Go to a dentist and get the best false teeth that money can buy. Don't do, as a working girl I knew once did, send sets of teeth to mother and sister and aunt for Christmas gifts because they were only $3 a set at a store.

Harry P.: You are suffering from a sick imagination. Fancy a man making himself nervous and ill imagining that the public is watching him and laughing at him. You have made a little tin god of yourself and, mounted on a little tin bicycle, you are careering around, watching the public and thinking it has eyes for no one but you. Dismount, little god, and roll away your wheel, and strip off your tin armour, and be a sensible little human worm, wriggling along with the rest of us.

Aurelius: Your list of your own attractions and accomplishments is singularly immodest. You send me samples of your "gifts." The verses are the merest twaddle. The Latin quotations are all wrong. The spelling is ludicrous. There is absolutely no grammar and your handwriting is simply frightful. The friends who tell you you are a genius do you a great wrong. You should resent it.

Jean: To marry the man a woman loves very much is a profound mistake. It is better for the man to be more in love than the woman. Where woman loves most tenderly, she is often apt to become a slave—this she cannot help for it is bred of great love. Few women can so control themselves to keep this great love a secret from the man. Once he knows the height and depth of it, he will value it lightly. When he is not too sure he is more attentive and loving. Satiety, as you know, is love's greatest enemy.

Bar the door upon him, Jean, and if you have it not, cultivate or feign indifference.

Little Woman: Asks is love eternal? Pray, how should I know? My experience of it has been that it is as ephemeral as the daily newspaper—and not as useful for it will not light kitchen fires. But then one is only an ordinary, middle-aged woman and such do not inspire love. My fairy prince, Little Woman, turned into a pumpkin stalk so long ago that I begin to believe he never existed as a prince, but was always a weed.

Crab Apple Tree: You have married a scamp who is a lazy, decrepit burden on you, and you are subject to the attentions of a kind fellow who pities your hard fortune. You must not encourage this friend: I advise you to maintain an attitude of severe reserve. Your inexpressibly hopeless letter reveals the dreariness of your wretched life. Don't fail now, however. Your release is at hand, for you tell me your husband is in the last stages of consumption, adding, sadly enough, "and he has no strength to kick me anymore." Help him through his final journey: it will give you something to do. And do not yield weakly to strong temptation after you have put up so gallant a fight.

Diogenes: So you scorn me as a "flighty gusher." Better that than a sour-soul-pickled misanthrope. Don't you know that cynicism without some leaven of simple kindness or pure "gush" never succeeds. Swift was a great man and students always read him, but he is regarded with a mixture of terror and hatred by ordinary people. I see you eying this column with a stony British stare, and then sitting down with malevolence on your brow, and gall in your pen, to flay me alive. Well, I won't be flayed. Pass on, brother, pass on, and find some more sensitive stock to lash with that blood-curdling pen of yours rather than a careless newspaper body who doesn't give a straw for your scoldings and cynical smiles.

Lucy: You must not go for the day's trip with the gentleman, nor to the opera. It is very mean to engage yourself to one man and go, unknown to him, about with another. If you deceive your lover, what will you do with your husband?

Violet: I cannot see why you should feel it necessary to sacrifice yourself to "comfort" a man for whom you do not care. You say "he kisses me, and I kiss him, and tell him I love him because he pleads so hard to hear it, but I do not love him." You are acting wrongly. You need a cold water douche; you have no right to go on like that. The young fellow will have every right to call you a jilt and a flirt. You think you'll marry him to "comfort" him. Some comfort you'd be!

Casey: No, it isn't nice for a girl to take presents from gentlemen friends, especially garters. Why, the very sound of it is enough! Don't ever do it, paper child; don't cost a man anything, not even street car fare.

Wooddyruwffy: I really think you ought to leave her alone. Women do not always marry men "for a comfortable living," you know. Sometimes they do care for their husbands.

E.L.G.: You are hard on the law and lawyers, friend. Why? Were you ever bitten? You are right, though, in asserting that a jury of women would, in any and all events, bring in a guilty were the prisoner a female. I can imagine the gusto which the lady jury foreman would roll the word out. Women are positively cruel to those of their own sex who are down. If there is a rupture between a married couple the women will invariably blame the woman. Why? Something to do with the sex-centres I suppose.

Philosopher: The old proverb says, "All things come to those who wait." Perhaps. But if one falls asleep while waiting, the good things pass one by. Wake up, Philosopher.

Kit's Child: I am going to be fearfully frank with you. You pursue me with letters on a most nauseous subject—the passion of a woman for a woman. It will land you in the madhouse. If you will not take this warning in time, the woe will be on your head. No more correspondence, please. I am disgusted.

Goosey: Dear, darling, simpleton. Your innocence is refreshing. So you wanted, oh, so badly, to kiss your adored Charles but was afraid of his whiskers. What a terrible situation. Did you fear abrasion of your charming complexion, or that tickling sensation, or what? Can't you persuade Charles to remove those horrid hirsute ornaments? Surely, he would do anything for his precious Goosey-Woosey.

Alice S.: The fellow is one of those cads who make men think of thick boots and walking sticks. You are foolish to notice him since you cannot thrash him. A good hiding is the only thing that would have any effect upon such a clumsy dolt.

J.J.: Poor woman, out in deep water, fighting the storm. And with little ones too! I know all about it, hapless soul, and I only pray that your heavily-freighted ship will make a good port someday.

Lady Betty: I am not dreadfully shocked at all but dreadfully sorry for you, poor, silly, shadow child. I would like to mother you for half an hour. You are drifting straight to ruin. You talk of "God's tempted ones," and yet you deliberately say you take delight in going on with the sin of your life. Remember, child, that punishment will come for it. You say you are safe from disgrace now. For how long? Have you any idea of the awfulness of that disgrace, of the consequences that may follow, of all the forlornness, loneliness and misery? Ah, Lady Betty, you are falling into a bottomless pit.

Jonathan: Do write simply. The inflation of your rhetoric is appalling. Your whole letter is (since you like strong words you shall have them) the most abstract bit of nebulous metaphysics I have ever received. You ask about a "remedy not derogatory to a sense of virility," regarding the punishment of your persecutors. Try a judicious course of punching their heads.

Misery: Writing letters by moonlight! We all do that sort of thing at certain times of our lives—moonstruck times. And you dropped tears? That was foolish. Oh, Lord, there's not a man in all the world who ever was or will be worth a woman's tears, except her father or son.

Melba: You are middle-aged, rich, not particularly handsome, nor clever, according to your own showing. And you ask me whether you should marry a boy of twenty-one. I find it difficult to be charitable and to call that deeply interesting youth a disinterested person. I have an inkling he has an eye on your money bags. Do not, I beg you, take into your comfortable life anything so jarring as a boy. You would rue it all your days.

Mary Foster: You are worrying yourself into insanity. To suppose that your husband is unfaithful to you because he offered to escort a woman home from your house, and because he always locks his desk before he goes out, is a trifle absurd. What would you have? A boor of a husband who did not know enough to behave in a mannerly way to a lady, or a ninny who was afraid to call his boots his own? Is the man to have no privacy at all? Must he leave every one of his papers loose for you to riot in? Suspicion is a defect of the brain, and not the heart. Root it out.

Woman-hater: Pray give women fair-play. We do gossip a great deal about trifles, but we are not so malignant and trivial as gossiping men are. Women can pass away the time chatting of dress and babies, and the iniquities of husbands and servants, but when male gossipers meet there is nearly always a dangerous flow of scandal. They toss the reputations of women up on the smoke of their cigars and no matter what a woman may have done, no man with a spark of nobility or breeding or manliness in him should talk of her at clubs. Men too often drop in low, sordid, contemptible babble. I would rather that the common laborer would blurt out his ill-saying of me over his pot of beer in the common barroom than that your gentleman of polish would bite at me with malicious word in his comfortable clubroom.

M.I.V.: Do not for a moment think that I wish to injure the reputation of High Park [in west-end Toronto] more than that of

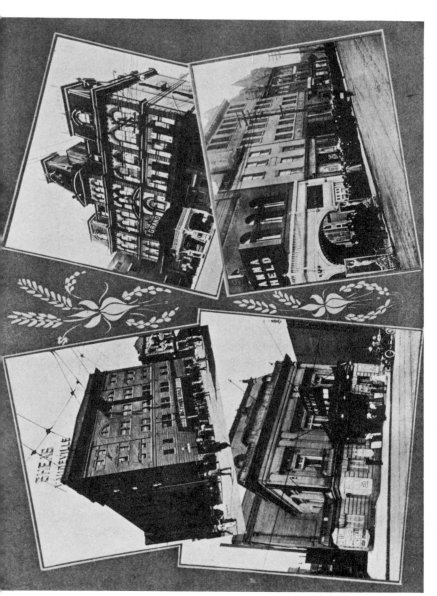

28. Four of Toronto's principal theatres at the turn of the century. (Ontario Archives)

29. World heavyweight cham
pion "Gentleman" Jim Corbe
(left) in 1897. Kit could s
little sense in watching "tw
men pound each other in
shapelessness." (The Bet
mann Archive)

30. Henry Irving and Ellen Terry, the famous English
acting team, in a scene from *The Vicar of Wakefield*.
The pair made seven North American tours between
1883 and 1904. (The Bettmann Archive)

31. Sarah Bernhardt in the role of Lady Macbeth (1884). Kit met the famous actress in Montreal in 1898. (The Bettmann Archive)

32. Lillian Russell, popular American singer and actress of the period, in a role from *Brigands*. (The Bettmann Archive)

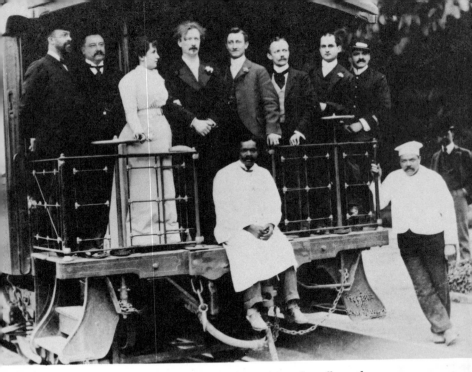

33. Mr. and Mrs. Ignaz Paderewski and staff on the rear platform of private railway car used during the pianist's American tour in 1900. Kit was more impressed with the virtuoso's "extraordinary reddish shock" of hair than with his playing. (The Bettmann Archive)

34. Lillie Langtry, English beauty and actress known as "the Jersey Lily." Kit interviewed her in Toronto in 1900. (The Bettmann Archive)

VOL. 15.   TORONTO, MONDAY, NOVEMBER 7, 1887   No 77

Grand Opera House,
TORONTO.

O. B. SHEPPARD,	- - - -	Manager.
O. H. SHEPPARD,	- - - -	Treasurer.
A. J. SMALL,	- - - -	Asst. Treasurer.

Engagement for Three Nights and Wednesday Matinee of

MRS. LANGTRY,

Accompanied by MAURICE BARRYMORE, and her
own Company in her Latest Success

—AS—

IN A LOOKING GLASS

CAST OF CHARACTERS.

Capt. Jack Fortinbras	Mr. Maurice Barrymore
Lord Udolpho Dayssay	Mr. Robert Hilliard
Count Paul Dromiroff	Mr. Frederick A. Everill
Sir Thomas Gage	Mr. H. A. Weaver
Algernon Balfour	Mr. Louis Calvert
Capt. Frank Fairfield	Mr. Sidney Herbert
Mons. Camille	Mr. George Raiemond
Major Roberts	Mr. Walter Lennox, Jr.
Lord Benley	Mr. W. Nicholson
Footman	Mr. William Spencer
Walter	Mr. Walter Plough
Norton	Mr. E. S. Percy
Kalmuck	Mr. M. Jones

Guests, Players, Detectives, Etc.

Lady Damer	Miss Hattie Russell
Miss Beatrice Vyse	Miss Kathrine Florence
Lady Gage	Miss Rose Roberts
Félicie	Miss Nadage Doree

—AND—

LENA DESPARD .... MRS. LANGTRY

SYNOPSIS OF SCENERY AND INCIDENTS.

ACT I.—Captain Fortinbras' Chambers in the Albany. The Game of Ecarté! Mrs. Despard or Mrs. Robinson? The Gambler and his victim. The quarrel and assault—Tableau.

ACT II.—A Drawing-room in the house of Sir Thomas Gage. Assembling of the Guests. The Charity Subscription—the price of a heart. Jealousy. The Defiance! "War to the bitter end." The Plot. The Broken Engagement—Animated Tableau.

ACT III.—The Casino at Monte Carlo at nightly. Brilliantly illuminated. The eager crowds at the Temple of Fortune. High Play. Lena breaks the bank. The Chief of La Troiceme Fection de la Chancelerie Imperiale. "I will take care of her and you too"—Tableau.

ACT IV.—Apartments in the Hotel de Brebant, Monte Carlo. The Robbery. The Old Bear. The Restoration. An old man's passion and despair. Lena's Resolve. Insolent demands of an unwelcome visitor. The Old Bear again—Tableau.

ACT V.—Lena's Boudoir in Balfour Castle, Scotland. Married to Algy. Arrival of Jack—plotter and accomplice ! The quarrel and exposure ! Dromiroff to the Rescue—"Too late ! Too late !" The Fatal Potion !—Affecting Tableau.

Mr. George Krock		Acting Manager
Mr. Jos. P. Reynolds	For Mrs. Langtry,	Business Agent
Mr. W. H. Young		Stage Manager
Mr. Harry Godbold		Machinist, Property Master

TUESDAY EVE.—"A Wife's Peril."
WEDNESDAY MAT.—"Lady of Lyons."
WEDNESDAY EVE.—"As in a Looking Glass."

THURSDAY, FRIDAY & SATURDAY,

COLVILLE'S "Taken From Life."

35. Playbill from the Grand Opera House, November 7,
1887, featuring Lillie Langtry and Maurice Barrymore.
(Metropolitan Toronto Library Board, Theatre Department)

36, 37. Evelyn Nesbit (left) and her husband Harry K. Thaw (below), accused murderer of Stanford White. Kit covered Thaw's sensational trial in New York in 1906. "Evelyn Nesbit has never known any deep emotion. She ran through the filth of life, grasping the money thrown to her with both hands. Her character appeared to be of a thickness of a sheet of notepaper." (The Bettmann Archive)

"KIT" HAS SAILED FOR SANTIAGO.

Left Key West Yesterday on the Red Cross Steamer Lampasas For the Battleground.

WAS BOUND TO GO THERE, AND HAS.

"Kit," the Mail and Empire's corre- | of Canadian backing—but everybody

38, 39. Headlines like these followed Kit's progress as she covered the Spanish-American War in the summer of 1898. (Ontario Archives)

PRICE TWO CENTS.

"KIT" REACHES CUBA'S SHORES.

Describes the Voyage, Undertaken After So Many Difficulties Had Been Surmounted.

HER EXPERIENCES ON A WARSHIP

Special to The Mail and Empire. | then silence would fall, and the ship,
On Board the Government Supply | lonely, sombre, an almost sentient

40. Kathleen "Kit" Coleman, 1864-1915. (Hamilton *Spectator*)

any other place on top of the earth. If I were to write of the shocking occurrences there, you would cry out against it as it was 'indecent.' How eager you seem to be to discredit my warning about the place. Very well. But when something dreadful happens, please remember that a warning was uttered in the public press against women wheeling alone or in couples in a park full of wild spots. You say you have seen "more in Riverdale Park to offend feminine sensibilities than ever in High Park while, as for the male escort, I think there is as much danger in taking a male companion along as there is in doing without one." Well, that is your opinion. I do not care to combat it.

Paula of the Broken Heart: It is hard to bear a man's blows in the heart, Paula. But let us be fair and acknowledge that women sometimes return them, with interest. Men and women are alike in these matters.

Mohammed: Do I think women will go to Heaven? Dear Turk, judging from a close study of men who are sharing quarters without the refining influence of my charming sex, I should say Heaven would be a sorry—and messy—place without them.

John Stanhope: Statistics do not bear out your statement that "women who lead the unfortunate life of the streets like that mode of life and, in spite of the horrors that have been pictured concerning it, are enabled by it to live in sinful luxury for years." The average life expectancy of the women on the streets in London from the day they start selling, their charms, until the day of their death is three and a half years. In spite of the preachers' ideas regarding it, "sinful luxury" does not often pay. Most of the girls die of wet feet, bad whisky, lack of sleep—and old age—before they are twenty-five. If some of the young girls who are thinking of this "sinful luxury" could be shown the end of it, they would turn away in horror from it, as they would from the pit of Hell were it gaping at their feet.

Arlene: We have not yet arrived at the era where women can propose marriage. Remember, paper child: man proposes, woman disposes.

Neglected: I feel quite certain that you are making your own misery. It is very considerate of your husband to go away while your fit of temper lasts. Some men would wrangle, but your husband's cool temper enables him to deal with a person of your sort very effectively. How silly you are! You have every comfort; your partner is kind, industrious and faithful, and yet you talk of going mad because the tired man turns his back to you at night and goes calmly to sleep instead of listening to your sentimental nonsense. It is fortunate for him that he can sleep through it all; otherwise it would be his madness you would be complaining about.

Ichabod: So you are going to be present at your ex-husband's marriage with another woman. Good heavens! "If the gods have no sense of humor, they must weep a great deal."

P.L.G.: Cease your loud belaboring. A hare is not caught with a drum.

L.G.R.: Do you think for a moment that you can judge the souls or hearts of men by their vocations? What a shallow view. There is not a man on earth who has not been moved by love. When some man takes his seat in the Senate, he is thinking of the backwoods school-marm who refused him when he was a boy, and how she will take it when she sees his appointment announced in the papers. All his life he has borne her in his mind and love has made him try to hurt her. Every author, every soldier, every man who tries to achieve anything has Love for his great mover. And you really think you see the real lives of men. Fool, you do not. No other human sees into the soul of his brother.

An English Violet: No, little flower, I am not always friendly to my dolls. Simply because these wooden and wax children who write to me pretend to be real human beings, which of course they are not. How could they be, seeing they are shadowy figures who creep to the dolls' post-office, some of them to drop disagreeable letters in the mail, merely because the mender of dolls happened to prick them with too sharp a needle?

15. AT HOME IN CANADY

It was a spirited fight. On one side, the businessmen and politicians wanting Canada to plunge into an economic union with the United States. Opposing them, the loyalists promoting the principle of a more independent nation, within the British Empire. A steadfast loyalist, Kit issued repeated warnings that the "grasping, land-hungry Yankees" had been "lusting after this country ever since John Adams declared in 1776, 'Canada must be ours.'" Like that equally resolute loyalist, Sir John A. Macdonald, Kit believed the pro-union spokesmen were almost preaching sedition. "I suppose a free-trade arrangement would increase profits," she said in 1890, "but what a price we are being asked to pay. Economic union would lead to annexation. For a few Judas-dollars, these mercenary profiteers would sell our grand nation and rob us of our unique identity." Kit was very familiar with that identity, having travelled from coast to coast. She found Nova Scotian fishermen "hard-muscled, romantic mist-figures," the Prairie farmer "as gentle and wordless as the soil he plows," and the average British Columbia woman "more British than the Queen." Her love of Canada—and her blatant anti-American streak—did not blind her to this country's faults. A private men's club, Nova Scotian hotels, and the way Canadians treated their writers all came under fire.

It's a pity there is not more patriotic spirit throughout the Dominion. Too busy, I suppose, in commercial ways but we will wake up someday. My! but I love Canada greatly.

Never yet, when on a visit to New York, have I failed to meet him—the man who would annex Canada in sixty days. He is usually a large, small-brained man whose bump of self-esteem is American and deformed. He is never a man of knowledge, refinement, manners. He has always "been in Canady" fishing near an Indian reservation. His idea of Canada is that she is small, mean and poor, mostly French and Indian, with "a sprinkling of Britishers" and "no spirit whatever."

He begins when he finds you are a Canadian, and especially when you are a woman, by bullying. "Come, now, what is Canady, anyway? A narrow strip of land without people, without a flag, without spirit or enterprise. Up there in Ottawa you've got a Parliament without a mind of its own, led by the nose by England. Everybody wears moccasins and jabbers in French. Why, when your Mackenzie came down to offer Canady to President Cleveland, he found Cleveland had gone fishing! That's all Cleveland thought of Canady. Why, we could take it in sixty days. We don't want it, M'am, we simply don't want it!"

"I'm glad to see you buying a Canadian magazine," said the old man who keeps the paper shop on the corner. "I'm always better pleased to sell Canadian productions than the others." If we all had as much esprit de corps as this vendor of news, Canadian literature might take on the speed of the snail, say, rather than proceed at its present tortoise pace. But there is no esprit de corps of that kind in Ontario. There is little encouragement to write. The home press either dismisses Canadian work entirely from its review columns or damns it with faint praise. Alas, one will find exhaustive reviews of the American magazines—*Munsey, Cosmopolitan, McClure's*—in Canadian papers but very trifling notices of the Canadian magazines.

The one great thing lacking throughout Nova Scotia is good hotels. They are building grand structures in many towns but, while paying much attention to size, outward appearance and furnishing, the main thing, the table, is utterly neglected. The food is generally poor to begin with; then it is ill-cooked. The people seem to be content with anything. Vile coffee, indifferent beef cooked until it is sapless, and very little fish, most of that smoked, varied by ham and eggs, seem to be Nova Scotia's staple diet.

Canada seems so good and pure when one is in the United States. The simple, strong Puritan faith, which I'm afraid I've laughed at sometimes—not in malice, God knows—seems such a sweet hedge about our fresh young country. One thinks of the Dominion as an old woman might think of a sweet nosegay of wild flowers, as something that grew very near to God.

The Toronto Club is too comfortable altogether. Such deep chairs for our lords to loll in, such cheery grate fires, such spacious, carpetted rooms, such luxuries of all kinds for the enjoyment of that great creature, Man, are too much for any poor woman, new or old, to gaze upon without a pang. I think it was a mistake to let us in. [Kit spearheaded a group of women journalists who got into the prestigious males-only club on the pretense that they were covering an art exhibit.] We shall know all about man's private paradise after this, and will resent his sitting under those palms on the piazza more than if we hadn't seen the luxurious place.

Half of the women who went there to assumedly look at the pictures were distracted from the gems of art by the amazing comfort of the place where Jack and Jim and Charlie take their ease. We were all particularly attracted by those sacred chambers which bore the weighty words, For Members Only, above their portals. Two of us begged for a peep, and beheld five scowling young men buried in deep chairs round a blazing fire. They looked as though they would have liked to send us women to a very hot place, and they said so with the windows of their souls; but we pretended to be New Women and stared stolidly back.

When we had sufficiently studied these young Blackbeards, we withdrew, sadder and wiser. Why can't we have such luxuries? Why isn't there a Woman's Club in Toronto where you and I, my friend, could bury ourselves in chairs and order cocktails and tell stories and smoke cigarettes. Of course, we would change the cocktails to tea and the cigarettes to candies, but we would still have those deep leather chairs left. Let us do something!

Of late years, weekly journals, petty magazines, strange woman's papers have sprouted up throughout Canada. Some grew from sproutings to twiglets of weak growth; others to the semblance of lean trees; a few into sturdy, if slender, young pines. A good many of these seedlings depended on the amateur writer for

food, and were willing to take anything by way of mental
pabulum. Hence their weak growth and early death.

No journal or magazine can be worthy of the respect, support,
or even toleration of any community if it starts on a non-paying
plan. A very serious injury is done thereby to professional writers
who cannot afford to give away brains by the yard, and a great
injustice is done to the community by asking it to subscribe to
stuff that cost the originators literally nothing beyond the expenses of paper and printing.

It is in Ottawa that you get the essence of the Canadian winter.
Winnipeg is too miserably cold; Toronto too damp; Montreal too
given to thaws; but Ottawa is the typical Canadian winter city
one used to read about long ago. The air is dry, bracing, in-
vigorating, like champagne. You see the most beautiful furs on
men and women; the sleighs are covered, nay, laden, with heavy
robes, and your driver looks like a bear or a huge raccoon. The
jingle of sleigh bells goes on all day, for they drive much in Ottawa.

I have been to every prominent Canadian city but not one of
them gives the delightful first impression that Ottawa does. The
stone houses look quaint, the streets, neither hilly nor flat, are not
the long reaches of houses that one is accustomed to, but twist
and turn, giving a sense of variety that is pleasant. Ottawa is altogether charming.

A Canadian sizing up American politics and condemning the
United States' pension system was met by this accurate summing
up of the pension list in Canada by the American: "Wal,
stranger," said the son of Texas, "I've been livin' in Canady for
sometime, and the only difference between the two countries is
that while the Government of the United States pensions off its
old soldiers, the Dominion Government spends most of its money
pensioning off political ward-heelers!"

An old Castilian legend has it that the Spaniards visited these
coasts before the French and, perceiving the barrenness of our
shores, without appearance of mines or riches, cried out, "Aca
nada." ("Here is nothing.") It is also said that the Spaniards

christened this country Capo di Nada (Cape Nothing), and that
gradually came the corruption to the word, Canada. Not flattering to us, is it? But it does go to prove that there may be nothing
in a name, and a very great deal in nothing.

Moosimin [Saskatchewan] in the evening, with the northern
lights in the sky. We watched them from the rear platform of the
flying train. A huge cone of light was hallowed in the roof of the
earth, and from its centre, slim, shivering ghosts of light flitted
across the sky, changing from luminous white to shifty blue, and
from that to palest, diaphanous green, and hence to a dull and
lurid red. Ragged fringes of quaking light trembled along the
edges of this giant cone, the stars shining through the mistiness
of them like diamonds in the blonde hair of a woman, and always this great umbrella of light followed the flying train,
roofing it. The heavens were streaked with stretching white
fingers, and the strange things danced a witches' dance far up in
the unknown, and a terror and awe took the souls of us as we
looked at the beautiful, lonely ghosts.

A New York journal prints the following: "Americans who go for
the first time to summer resorts in Canada are surprised to find
how many such places exclude Canadians. The reason given is
that many Americans prefer not to meet Canadians upon intimate terms such as summer hotels or boardinghouse life must
commit them to. Though the hotel proprietors are themselves of
the provinces, they encourage patronage from the States and
debar their own people. The dictum, 'They don't take Canadians,' seems to give a house a certain cachet. A colony of fashionable Baltimoreans, who for years have repaired for the summer to North Hatley, Quebec, pride themselves upon never
having admitted a Canadian within the hotel limits." How
funny! When we Canadians are looking everywhere for places
that exclude the ubiquitous American!

Thomas Edwards, Leeds, Eng.: You belong to a class which,
though eminently respectable, is not wanted here in Canada.
You wish to go to Manitoba. Very well. You arrive, you go to
Winnipeg, you stay at the Queen's Hotel. You meet plenty of

Englishmen like yourself, who have a bit of capital, and like them you proceed to spend it. When your money is gone on drinks you look for work. You will walk the streets day after day. You will wait in line at the CPR office. You will ask at hotels if bookkeepers or clerks are needed. You will even take a job as a hotel runner; you will be glad of a quarter for sweeping snow off house steps or bucking wood at seventy-five cents a day. You may drift into railway labor or carrying planks at a sawmill; in the summer, you may be a milker of cows on a farm. Only men of good trades or agricultural workers are wanted in Canada. Do not swell the numbers of the young men who mistakenly feel Canada is an El Dorado.

M. R. Niven, London, Eng.: Don't send the lads to Canada. It is such half-educated young men with no aptitude (as you yourself acknowledge) for useful work who are the nuisance of our colony. We don't want town-bred clerks who have never used their hands at anything bolder than cricket. Ours is a young country, but we go in for work, real, earnest, hard work. Rose-leaves do not make bedding in Canada. Sickly, indolent, feeble lads, who can do nothing at home, should not be sent to a country which demands manhood and strength. For that matter, neither is Canada a convict colony, where the diseased and criminal can be sent off to, as one sends garbage to a nuisance ground.

With many groanings, and whisperings, and bumpings against the wharf [Kit was on a steamer docking after a trip from Vancouver in 1894], we came upon Victoria, sitting on the edge of Vancouver Island, her lights gleaming like eyes, her breath perfumed like flowers, her streets wet and slippery from recent rains. So suggestive of England was Victoria that twice on the way to our hotel we had to look around, wondering where we were. Not in Canada, surely! And, doubtless, if you asked one of the "natives," he would reply, "Certainly not. This is British Columbia!"

A quaint and beautiful old-world city it is. Far in runs the sea, in bays and inlets, between precipitous cliffs backed by high and rugged mountains which are covered with fir and hemlock and cedar. Hilly are the streets of this English town; many and handsome are the buildings, like its handsome climate that fascinates one from "down East." Like that of England it is, without an awful east wind; flowers all year round, Torquay of the Pacific. English even to the winding lanes; English, of course, as to accent, and highly English in remittance men. A superabundance of "r's" and a lack of "h's"; a well-sustained "rainy season" and "knickers," and a profound contempt for "Canadians." Slow, solid, sure Victoria is like her namesake, our gracious Majesty.

Lovely are the complexions of the women—Old Country complexions suggestive of underdone beef and quaffings of beer, but delicious to look upon, rosy and healthy. A year back are the ladies of Victoria in fashion, for ladies here wear high and narrow shoulder puffs and "sailor's" hats, and the hair is worn bun fashion. A lovely place to wear out last season's clothes: what does it matter if the hat is out of a date before the flood when cheeks are rosy, eyes bright, and life an easy-going jog-trot towards eternity, as it certainly is in slow, happy Victoria, B.C.

It is not perhaps desirable for a woman to dogmatize on these things but it seems to me there is room in Canada for development companies built on somewhat different lines than those that usually prevail—companies composed of small capitalists who are also workers. The company of the present day is usually a combination of the idle rich, who strive to grab everything in sight, and to make the poorer people work for them. It is conceivable that co-operation might be introduced into the business of settling the magnificent vacant lands of this country, in a way that would create a sort of independent yeoman class, who would no longer be subject to the slavery in which Capital is gradually enmeshing the greater part of the population.

Independence is such a precious gift that it is strange that more young men do not determine to possess it. On the contrary, there is a constant crowding into the cities and a frittering away of youth and vigor on pursuits that lead to nothing. Our governments are too busy helping rich people to bestow much attention on the rank and file. A company of capitalists who wish to grab a few thousand acres or some rich seams of coal are given every attention, but a score of bona-fide workers who might, on a co-operative principle, develop a modest tract of country would find it exceedingly difficult to get any help from the powers that be. Yet it is on the developing of this country in an agricultural way that its future depends. Anyone who for a serious second thinks on the subject must see how important the creation of these worker-dominated co-operative companies could be to Canada's growth and prosperity.

16. DOWN SOUTH IN YANKEELAND

Sir John A. Macdonald's last hurrah came in 1891. Campaigning on a platform defending Canada-U.S. trade barriers, the aging Tory chieftain thumped Laurier and his Liberals at the polls. (Laurier had to wait another five years before he gained office.) The victory reassured Macdonald that Canada, only twenty-four years into Confederation, had the will to survive as a nation: in the 1880s one million Canadians—roughly one quarter of the population—had fled to the United States in hope of finding better living conditions. The population drain was curbed in the 1890s by, among other factors, increased natural resource development and the spreading realization that America, far from being a streets-of-gold paradise, was beset with poverty and violent clashes between workers and the ruling class. The expression "the Gay Nineties" was, in truth, a misnomer. The decade may have been gay for John D. Rockefeller, Andrew Carnegie, J. P. Morgan, George Pullman, and the other financial czars who controlled much of the American economy, but immigrants often had to live in squalid ghettos, working for $1.00 a day in a time when eggs costs twenty-two cents a dozen and butter twenty cents a pound.

In her column, Kit did all she could to persuade Canadians to stay at home. Still, she did little to dispel the illusion that the United States was a more glamorous place to be than stodgy, unimaginative Canada. If anything, she unconsciously contributed to it. For news of American cultural, scientific, and medical advances were sure to earn space in "Woman's Kingdom," and Kit admitted she would have paid her own fare, if need be, to sit in on the Thaw trial or to cover the World Columbian Exposition in Chicago. In spite of her anti-U.S. bias, Kit was utterly fascinated by American personalities and events, and hardly a year passed that she did not make at least one trip into the depths of Yankeeland.

It is almost with a feeling of despair that one takes pen in hand to attempt a description of this stupendous work [the Columbian Exposition, 1893] this White City filled with the riches, arts, refinements of the world. You go there prepared to see wonderful things, expecting to see a lot of things that are tawdry and fake too, but you are not in the least prepared for the reality.

This White City, lying in the sun by her wide lake, with her graceful Grecian columns, her stretches of white buildings, her lagoons and islands and fantastic woods, is a revelation. It is all so gigantic, so very beautiful, that one can only compare it with the Arabian Nights.

On first entering the Fair grounds one is struck by a weird, depressing feeling of powerlessness, as though there was almost too much to explore. You feel you never will be able to walk those vast distances, stocked with all that is most lovely and curious—the gathered art of centuries, the rich stuffs of Eastern bazaars, the paintings, sculpture, inventions and curios of ages and ages.

The Midway is the place to saunter of the evening when you tire of State buildings and are brain-wearied with scientific, historical and artistic research. Nearly all the foreign element congregate on the Midway. You jostle by bare-legged Arabs in loose garments, and Turkish gentlemen in fez and wide silken trousers. Gay dancing girls, Syrian maids, and Arab boys trot gaily down to where the railway takes you round curves, up hills and down slopes at break-neck, toboggan speed for ten cents, or to the giant Ferris wheel with its three thousand colored incandescent lights, which takes you in passenger cars up until you can see not alone Chicago and her suburbs but parts of the states of Wisconsin, Michigan and Illinois.

On the Midway you can listen to the pipe-playing of Bedouins, wearing sandals. You can see the beauties of the harem of a Moorish palace. From an Irish Village it is but a step to where South Sea Islanders can scarcely be induced to retain their modest wrapping of a sheet for which they can see no necessity; the little brown women of Java are waiting to offer you their small, limp hands and to show you, in their pretty, childish way, how they weave their fantastic hats of straw. Fakes, you will say. No, there may be a few fakes in the Fair, but these foreign people are real. They are not Irishmen picked up in New York and painted black or brown, and tricked out in strange costumes. Neither are they foreigners who live in this country. Real Nubians from Nubia, real Syrians from Syria.

At night, when the vast buildings are flooded with electric light, and the great electric fountains are tossing clouds of crimson and gold and pale pink up to a distance of one hundred and fifty feet, when the beading of the incandescent globes starts along the edges of the domes and towers and cupolas, when you go in gondolas under bridges, as you would in Venice—it is then that the beauty of White City comes to you—as the realization of many a dream.

As she had with Cassie Chadwick, Kit tried to obtain an exclusive interview with Harry Thaw. She pretended that she was the accused slayer's sister but the New York jail authorities were not fooled and she was stopped at the front door. So Kit had to content herself with covering part of the trial. Thaw, a flamboyant playboy with $40 million in his bank account, had murdered Stanford White, the wealthy architect reponsible for building Madison Square Garden, in 1906. Thaw informed the police that he was avenging the wrong done to his petite, dimple-faced bride, Evelyn Nesbit. White, a middle-aged libertine, had set her up in a Manhattan love nest when she was sixteen. A chorus girl and actress from a Philadelphia slum, Nesbit had fled the love nest to marry Thaw.

The press corps generally depicted Nesbit as a hapless, misled victim of her own beauty, entangled in a web by two lecherous millionaires. Not Kit. She raked her over the coals, saying she was a "Broadway waif who would rather do wrong for a few yards of velvet, a handful of lace, a supper at Rector's, than work for a decent living and room in a cold backroom of a New York boardinghouse."

The jury was split at the first trial. A second trial was held and Thaw, pleading insanity, was sent to a mental institution. The final Thaw verdict brought Kit's anti-American feelings to the

surface. "In America, the land of commercial greed and fake pa-
triotism, money rules the day and, seemingly, the courts. Any-
body can escape the hangman, so long as that anybody is an
American millionaire."

The Thaw case has got New York in its grip. Everywhere it is
discussed. The newsstands are cleared of the latest editions almost as soon as they appear. In the cars, on the subway, in res-
taurants, even on the streets, all are reading the Thaw trial. It is
the main topic of conversation at boarding-house tables and the
opinions of some of the women told out loud would shock and
frighten even a world-worn woman. Never did Gotham appear
so sordidly immoral.

I spent two days at the trial during the cross-examination of
Evelyn Nesbit. Your first impression of her as she ascended the
witness stand would likely be one of sympathy, with her amazingly youthful and pathetic appearance, and her fragile beauty.
As you hear her testimony, practical common sense rather
changes that first idea. She is small and slender. Her face,
framed in cloudy dark hair, is a pure oval, refined and delicate.
The eyes are long, dark, heavily-lashed and appealing. The
mouth rich and full, the chin weak.

She excites your pity and sense of maternal caringness. Her
voice is high-pitched, rising at times to shrillness. Her dress is an
admirable one for the occasion. The simple velvet hat, with its
bunch of violets; the hair tied in a low knot on her neck, the simple blue dress with the little schoolgirl jacket belted high up
under the arms. This little Broadway gamine soon reveals herself
as a mercenary. Out for the "good" things her youth and beauty
could buy, and out for the highest bidder, this young woman
plainly showed herself to be. The New York newspaper women
are writing reams of sentimental rubbish about her. Evelyn Nesbit, you felt, has never known any deep emotion. She ran
through the filth of life, grasping the money thrown to her with
both hands. Her character appeared to be of a thickness of a
sheet of notepaper.

How far is she to be blamed? Perhaps not at all. If we believe
in environment, which we surely must allow has an effect on the
moulding of character, we might well hold this street gamine in-

nocent of evil intention. Her mother—perhaps the most despised woman in New York today—is one of those who drift from one Tenderloin boarding-house to another—often without means to pay the board—lazy, loving the good things and weighted down with two children she could barely support herself. She taught the child early that she was beautiful; to go out and earn for her and her brother. She asked no questions when she saw her trailing Worth gowns, the diamonds, the electric cabs. She even shared in them, in the St. Regis dinners, the Rector suppers. As she stands in public opinion today, she is a mother who sold her child on the open market to the highest bidder.

District Attorney Jerome is by long odds the greatest figure in the trial. He dominates the whole court-room. Restless, pacing to and fro in the small space before the judge, he snaps out question after question in rapid-gun fire. His square jaw, cold eye, aggressive attitude, but above all else the sardonic grin on his face when his witness denies, "does not remember," or otherwise evades what you read on his face to be the truth, are almost terrifying. You feel he could wrest any admission from you were you under his cross-examination. But the pale-faced girl answers him coldly, steadily. At times when some peculiar query she is in fear of is fairly shot at her by the District Attorney, she grows as white as she will be when she is lying in her coffin.

Jerome is dramatic. He will jump away from the subject in hand to some apparently irrelevant matter, then in a flash come back with a vital question. Mr. Delmas, on the contrary, is a small, fatherly-looking man, courtesy itself. His attitude toward the witness is gallant, even chivalrous, as is, I imagine, his attitude toward all women. He is like a mild Napoleon in appearance. His voice, rich, deep, persuasive, is in sharp contradiction to that of Jerome, which is grating, harsh, raucous. A distinctly magnetic man of strong personality, yet not half as fascinating as sombre Jerome.

Judge Fitzgerald seems almost a misfit at this extraordinary trial. He is fat, with a turn-up humorous nose and a decidedly Celtic cast of countenance. He is a man of moods. He is extremely fussy at one time, calm at another. He sounds irascible at times, gentle at other times. He is a splendid subject for caricature—yet he has a good heart, and it is said Jerome would rather have had any other judge of the Criminal Court than Judge Fitzgerald.

There remains one more prominent figure to speak of. Harry Thaw is a big man with an extremely ugly and exceedingly unintelligent face. His head is badly shaped, eyes protruding, mouth high, and lips set over yellow teeth. His hair is shaggy, his face a grey-yellow. He suggests the degenerate. He sits facing the witness stand with his counsel all about him. He stares at his wife with those protruding brown eyes; then suddenly swings sideways with a jerking movement; whispers to his counsel, swings back again, and busies himself with his papers, among which his long, white, nervous hands move restlessly.

He does not look quite sane. He looks at times as if he would like to shoot Jerome. Again, an idiotic grin spreads over his ugly face. He suggests the idiot rather than the raging madman. But, perhaps, he has gone through enough to drive many a man insane. You make excuses for him in your own mind—as you make excuses for many of the actors in this awful play of life—yet, as you rise and pass out into the darkening streets, the thoughts that pursue you are of a little mercenary, a satyr of genuis, and a big broad-faced fool.

So they are turning old goats into young ones in Chicago! The pilgrimage to Lourdes will not be in it with the exodus of old men from all parts to that city. "The return to youth"—so reads the news report—"is produced by hypodermic injections of the lymphatic fluid of animals, particularly of young goats." Further on we learn that "Dr. Hawley administered injections of the fluid from the lymphatic glands to a dog known to be fourteen years old," and, at the end of two months, "the dog was as lively as a puppy."

This is alarming news, since they do not apply the rejuvenating power to women. Are old women to remain decrepit and aged while their ancient consorts endow themselves with the sportive inclinations of a young goat? I find this distressingly immoral. The modern Faust no longer need put himself to the expense of selling his soul to the Devil; all he will do is take the train to Chicago, a decorous, dignified greybeard, and return a frisky young fellow, full of gambols and wickedness. Imagine the

consternation of the old ladies! Inspector Archibald of the
Toronto police ought to detail someone to watch the outgoing
and incoming trains and so prevent an immoral epidemic from
pervading this good, moral, well-behaved city.

A correspondent to this column today proclaims his immediate
departure for fields Elysian. "I shall take a contingent of Canadian goats with me," he writes, "seeing that they are number one
quality." Well, anything would be better than the Yankee-goat
spirit. Its gambols would cost this city too much in alterations
and repairs. Besides, it would incite to jingoism. If our Canadian
elderly gentlemen are to be inoculated with goat-like youth, by
all means let it be done in a loyal, Canadian spirit. Canada for
Canadians! Canadian goats for elderly Canadian gentlemen! But
what are we ladies to do? Are there no lambs that might, for a
consideration, remit their gentle qualities to elderly women? Can
not we who are past our youth be inoculated with the sweet
bleatings and playful gambollings of Mary's little pet? Or must
we always, like sad Gretchen, be taken in by the machinations of
Faust and the Devil?

The burrows under Chinatown in San Francisco have been
revealed by the recent great disasters [1906]. Tourists who were
taken around Chinatown by guides at an immense fee rarely saw
these underground places, some of them two or three storeys underground, where women burned like trapped rats. The earth-
quake and the fire have laid all bare.

But there is nothing left to see save the human rat-holes where
people lived strange, silent, awful lives. I went through them
with Chief of Police Crowley and two of his men. What a
repellent place, with its stinking odours, its noiseless, secretive,
watchful people who glided about the dim lanes and passages
like ghosts. How old, how squalid, how terrible were the in-
tricacies of the place. It would take the pen of a Dickens to
describe it.

A mass of narrow streets and courts to which mouldering balconies and stairways led. Along the balconies we went, now
stumbling up and down unseen steps, now stooping past a low
entry, now in darkness, now in half-light; passed by slinking men
in blouse and pig-tail; starting in affright when from some black

doorway a head was thrust as we passed by. So, up and down creaking stairs and into a room where two white girls lay in bunks and far off in a top bunk, by himself, a villainous-looking old man lay smoking opium.

Not a word was spoken. It was like being in a charnel house. No one took any notice of us, save that one of the girls pulled a frowsy blanket over her head. The old Chinaman took no heed of us at all. He was off somewhere, haply away with the Heavenly Mandarin, listening to the wise words of hoary old patriarchs—gone from the squalor here to the glory there.

Down in New York the Four Hundred have departed from the Jenness-Miller school and are flocking to Delsarte. Mrs. Whitney set the Delsarte ball rolling in ultra-fashionable circles by introducing the study of its methods in her drawing-room last winter. Illustrating the Delsarte method, Mrs. Henrietta Russell gave lessons in grace, expression and pose. Mrs. Russell is, in fact, the latest apostle of physical culture, and her girls return to their homes looking with pitying eyes on their ungainly friends who have never been taught how to walk, sit, breathe, or go up the stairs properly.

And how is it done? First, dear girls, the prophetess teaches her pupils to become as limp as a wilted lettuce; nothing can be done with you unless you "decompose" yourself. Why should pretty, fresh young girls indulge in an exercise that smacks of an over-ripe corpse? Because vanity conquers repugnance. I had the pleasure of seeing forty women (myself included) "decomposing" themselves. We were all reduced to mush. Not one of us owned a backbone; we leaned forward with shoulders humped up, and sideways with a pathetic droop; some of us grovelled and wallowed in the depths of limpness. After the course ended, we would be fit to annihilate the male animal's resistance: he would grovel at our feet while we, angelic creatures that we would become, could extend a Delsartean hand, raising him to heights of delicious bliss.

Mrs. Russell stood before us in a loose Bernhardty drapery, which jeered at our tailor-made gowns, our squeezed-in waists, our padded busts. "Now, ladies," she said, "this exercise has put you in a receptive state, and you are ready to breathe." Good gracious, I thought, have I never breathed all these years? Have I been able to fulfill functions such as motherhood, and am only now being taught how to inhale? Alas, it was so. We had imagined along with the rest of mankind that there was such a thing as woman's natural grace. We were told that the average woman wobbles when she walks, squats when she sits, falls in a bundle when she faints, and tangles skirts around her ankles when she kneels and prays. Worst of all, not one of us knew how to breathe properly. Henrietta taught us: we would forever more breathe from the abdomen. It was more mannerly to breathe that way at social gatherings and, she said, better for the figure as well.

We next learned how to sit down in a chair, a process that took fully five minutes. Then we learned how to say our prayers gracefully. First you decompose yourself, becoming as limp as you can, then with swaying waist and hips drop softly on one knee; after a few moments in this position, let down your other knee, gently, kicking the skirts out behind you. Take your pocket handkerchief and slowly, with eyes upturned, let your face subside into the handkerchief, and remain buried in profound grief for your sins. For three minutes there must be no peeping out of the corner of your eye; that's vulgar, Mrs. Russell said.

The Delsartean method rules New York women. They want Mrs. Russell to criticize their figures, dress, style, etc., and they follow her advice faithfully in all respects save one—they cannot be induced to part with their beloved corsets. Women will always fall prone to the idol of the moment; next month, when a newer, more chic idol appears, the Delsarte school, Henrietta Russell and her physical antics will fade from Four Hundred memory, or be spurned and despised by them, as they lie veiled and prostrate before some equally ludicrous and faddey image, whose mission in the cosmopolitan centre is to guile the rich and pocket their almighty dollars.

A prig is a man or woman who overdoes their duty, and prigs, and all their family—cads, snobs, etc.—are very hateful people. A prig is not necessarily a bad person; just the opposite, for he is generally too good: one gets too much of him, he is a frightful bore who fails to realize the fact. He is not even a hypocrite, that is, not a conscious one; but, oh, how he does make one yawn; what an excellent sleeping draught he is did he but know it. Verily, even a prig hath his uses.

And what great men were atrocious prigs. Look at the mightiest and most renowned of all prigs—the man who founded the greatest State ever known, who stood steadfastly against England, who never told a lie—George Washington. What an awful boy immaculate George must have been. A boy who never told a story, not even a 'white lie' about being late for school, or playing truant, or anything. Gracious! I think as much as I am against corporal punishment, I'd have whipped a bit of human nature into that impossible boy.

A curse in the bay, where the wind-darkened waters sweep in softly; long lines of flowering, hanging gardens; grave hills standing closely round, on eternal guard; a vast red pile of buildings, barred and walled, and thirteen hundred human beings held fast behind stout iron gates—this is San Quentin.

We came to it across the beautiful Bay of San Francisco, and the boat twisted and curved in among the hills and wide bends till the hoarse scream of the waiting train made her strain in puffing hurry to the wharf. A short spin by rail, a shorter drive by stage, and the State prison of California lay shining in the sun before us.

The first thought that came to mind was the astonishing difference between this beautiful place and those other prisons we had visited—terrible Newgate, black and cavernous, filled with ghastly legends and ghastly relics; grey Woking, barren and dismal; the vast prison of St. Petersburgh where, if stones could speak, it would be in trembling whispering of secret, awful doings. The second thought was of how little all the brightness and beauty was compared with glorious liberty. A prison is always a prison, even if one is caged in a palace, and maybe the very riot of sunshine and flowers, the exquisite freshness of the golden mornings, the soft, cold starlit beauty of the California nights, added ten times to the torture of imprisonment seen, as they were, through heavy bars.

We entered the black iron gates and came upon a courtyard inside that was one huge rose garden. The prison buildings line this court. No woman is ever allowed within that portion of the prison—by far the largest portion—set aside for men, so we had to content ourselves with going through the women's quarters. We entered several cells and talked with the women. There was a girl, a wan and pinched-looking creature, busy at knitting, whose face lighted for a moment at the sight of the matron and me. Serving a long sentence for vitriol throwing, she was hoping for a new trial—hoping against hope. Her face fell, as she said it, into the same dull, despairing expression, and she bent to her work again, the sun lingering in the room she had made bright with pictures and ribbon bows on the walls.

We closed the door and passed on. The sound of a baby crying was surely a strange sound in this weary place. She was a pale young thing, the mother, only twenty-three and in for twenty-five years for murder. A slim figure in a black gown, a tangle of red hair, a face with a dazed look as though not rightly comprehending why she was here or what she had done. She had shot the man who had ruined her, at the bidding of her husband. The baby, four months old, was leaping in her arms. They would take it from her, when it was weaned, and she would have to serve out the years alone.

A wild clamoring from a cell further down; a noise of singing and coarse talking. She was locked in this one, a murderess, in for life, and the terror of the matron and the other prisoners. We could see her peering at us behind the bars, and her coarse voice rang out, "Peek-a-boo!" A colored woman who would regain her liberty in a month's time was making shirts in the next cell. How different it was for her! For hope was there and all the gladness that hope brings.

A few other women, about sixteen in all, comprised the prisoners. Their lot seemed harder than that of the men, who are frequently sent outside the prison to work in neighboring gardens and houses, and who have a wide, sunny court to exercise in. The women never get outside their narrow yard, the dreary corridor, the bare cells. To be there for life! Never to see anything more; to tramp eternally up and down the same long passage; to sit always behind the same barred windows. Let us out, we said hurriedly, to the matron.

Principle is a great thing. Because of it, I have not seen a copy of the *Mail* for many days, have not received a letter. We are tied-up in San Francisco by the biggest strike this continent has ever known. [The strike grounded Kit after she visited San Quentin in 1895.] There are two factions fighting, the railroad magnates and the railroad employees, and the public is standing between them getting all the blows.

Strikes are splendid things as long as they do not effect our own immediate necessities. When a woman has her trunks packed for home, her ticket ready to be nipped, her last washing paid for and packed, and a flood comes along and washes out the railroad, she submits to the "visitation of God," unpacks the top layer of her trunk, and prays for patience. But when the floods are dried, and all is made ready, and a fight comes along among railway people, and trains are tied-up, and the boats crowded nearly to sinking, and no letters, alack, but there comes upon a woman a keen regret that in her youth she did not learn the cuss language which seemingly gives such relief to the aggrieved souls of men. So she sits on her trunk and shakes mittened hands at departing and groaning ships, and shakes her parasol at rusting cowcatchers, and is filled with a mighty wrath.

Having had our grumble out, let us put in time looking at strikes in general. How many people understand the second chapter of Exodus? That first "strike" was a great one. King Menetaph, the Pharaoh in the Bible, must have been a poltroon. So cruelly did he oppress those foreigners in Egypt that they all turned out on strike. Six hundred thousand Israelites refused to work any longer, and determined to leave the hated country. They stole off in the night towards the Red Sea and the King said he had a dream which commanded him to lead his cavalry in pursuit. His notion of leading his cavalry was much like Mr. Pullman's in the present disturbance—to run away and leave his lieutenants to fight it out for him. Pharaoh, at least, went far enough to see the tidal wave engulf his horsemen and then he returned, like a beaten dog, to dwell in loneliness.

This was the first big strike; the next was that of the Roman slaves. We have been going on at it until the present day—and probably all women will soon strike against housekeeping, motherhood and raising babies! A word as to both sides in the railroad dispute. Loads of fruit have been ruined, live freight starved, the mails stopped, and dying men have gone out without a last word from wife or mother who were summoned to them on short notice. Distress and discomfort prevail. What is the cause? Monopoly, they cry. In place of Pharaoh, we have set up a capitalist who rules over a vast army of laborers. For some reason or other, he sees fit to cut down wages. Naturally, the workers resent this and strike.

Seventy years ago, the demands of strikers were emphasized by the burning of stacks and the smashing of machinery. The men of today think it is enough to walk in processions and to make speeches. The means of action differ but the problem is the same. The problem will only be solved when there is co-operation between capital and labor—and not till then. It is noticeable how fast the aristocrats, the class who were wont to be drones, are coming into sympathy with the poor. The religious class, the class who used to be wrapped up in ceremonies, have in many cases become active too. Still capital has an iron hand, and its blow falls upon labor. Yet labor stands up defiantly, risking those blows, and her ranks are deep and firm.

And what has all this to do with me? Well, it has much to do, this strike, with a woman who is sitting on her trunk waiting for a train to transport her to the decent Dominion where such warring is unknown. Co-operation? If I had my way I would wed capital and labor tomorrow and knock the monopolists on their heads while doing so. Still, though it is hard waiting—Hurrah for the laborers!

17. OFF TO THE WARS

The sinking of the U.S. battleship Maine *in Havana harbor in February 1898 prompted President William McKinley and the Congress to declare war on Spain, which was already struggling to suppress a revolutionary uprising in Cuba. The American involvement drew top-line reporters from around the world to Florida and eventually Cuba itself; Richard Harding Davis, Stephen Crane and Frank Norris were among them.*

Kit resolved to join the press corps in spite of a ban imposed on women journalists by the U.S. military. She journeyed to Washington and bulldozed her way through a crowded anteroom into the office of Secretary of War Russell Alger. He burst out laughing when she said she wanted to go to Cuba. It was no place for a woman, he said, because, among other things, soldiers would be wandering around their camps with their shirts off. Kit returned to his office again and again until he gave in and signed papers making her the only accredited woman correspondent among 134 males. (Two American women, Anna Benjamin of Leslie's *magazine and Katherine Trumbull of the* Chicago Record, *went to Cuba too. Neither was accredited. Benjamin became a Red Cross nurse and Trumbull crossed the water on a coal collier. Both sent back periodic reports that fell far short of Kit's stories in color and depth.)*

Kit stayed six weeks in a humid, insect-ridden Tampa hotel with other reporters waiting for a Cuba-bound ship. Charles H. Hand of the London Daily Mail *wrote a feature on her, telling how indignant the male reporters were at having her there. "What kind of a newspaper proprietor was it, who would send a tenderly-nurtured lady around amidst the hardships, the bullets, the yellow fever germs of a Cuban war?" Hand asked. The British journalist and his colleagues were surprised that shortly after she got to Florida Kit visited the U. S. Army encampment and came back "introducing us to generals and colonels." He confessed that the indignation ceased when Kit scooped them all with a story on a secret arms shipment being dispatched to the Cuban rebels.*

When the special press boat departed for the battered island, it left without Kit. The army commander, Brigadier General William B. Shafter, refused to let a woman on board despite her credentials. "I'm going through to Cuba and not all the old generals in the old army are going to stop me," Kit proclaimed in print.

Even the Red Cross ship leaving Key West turned her down. Clara Barton, the Red Cross head, disliked Kit on sight. But Kit made it to Cuba. She talked her way onto a decrepit U.S. government freighter carrying war supplies and, as it always did when she was on a foreign assignment, her newspaper bally-hooed her exploits in black headlines: "Kit Follows the Course of the Escaping Spaniards"; "Kit Talks to the Wounded"; "Kit Visits the Camp of Teddy's Terrors"; "How Kit, Mounted on a Mule of High Degree, Inspected the Troops."

The U. S. Army made few allowances for Kit's presence. She had the occasional pup tent to herself, and she slept in buildings commandeered by the military, but mostly she bedded down on the bare earth, putting straw or clothing beneath her. She ate where and when she could, with the brass, with soldiers, with Cuban peasants, and one of the cherished possessions in her battered kit bag was the bar of soap she used while bathing in streams and beside farmyard wells. Kit did not write of the actual battles, which she viewed from a safe distance, but of the events and people in the background. Her writing was marvelously vivid. Spanish soldiers in a field hospital were "living ghosts of men" with "eyes sunken far in their sockets burning like lamps on the edge of extinction." After the crucial battle at Santiago, Kit stated, "Here in Santiago, men, nobles and commoners alike, dying in filth and stench, and uttermost squalor; lying out there on the hills for the buzzard and the crab to feed upon. There was heartbreak in the thought of it; in the sight of all this hopeless suffering. We are very little creatures. Very small and cheap and poor."

After a month on the island, Kit returned to the United States on a troop ship, helping to nurse wounded soldiers. General Alger asked her to go on a lecture tour, billed as the world's first female war reporter. She agreed to address the International Press Union of Women Journalists in Washington, D.C., but she balked at a nation-wide tour. "If I tell the women of the United States the awful things I have seen," she said, referring to green, young soldiers the U. S. Army used as cannon fodder, "you will have riots on your hands."

As it did to so many soldiers, war changed Kit. She had gone to Cuba thinking it would be a great adventure; it was, but the war also wrought great horrors that thoroughly appalled her. She vented her feelings in a piece on the Russo-Japanese War of 1904-5. Kit seldom drew in her claws on any issue, so it was surprising to find her suppressing her strong anti-war beliefs in a 1900 military story. Canadian troops were departing for the Boer War front and, perhaps leery of being accused of disloyalty, she turned in a highly colorful tale that put a stamp of approval on the entire venture.

Blazing under the sun lay Santiago. A city of mean streets. A city spread out on the edge of a foul harbor, lying in the lap of grey-green hills, beautiful at the first glance, horrible in its squalor and stench when you come close to it. A city four hundred years old, inexpressibly quaint, inexpressibly filthy. [Kit toured Santiago a few days after it capitulated.]

The wide street which runs along the water's edge was crowded with an odd mixture of men and beasts. American and Spanish soldiers lounged about, Uncle Sam's boy, in an almost ragged uniform comparing ill as to sartorial effect with the Dons in their clean blue drills. In vain I looked for the poorly-clad Spanish soldier one had read so much of in the newspapers. It was "our" boys who were looking uncared for, ill, worn and seedy.

Everywhere waggons, pack mules, government stores, Red Cross packages. It is difficult to pick one's way along the wharf. Big bales of hay piled on the ground; mule spans of six or eight animals; boxes, barrels of potatoes that, already decaying, send up their stench to mingle with the other foul odours. All these, and a thousand other things lie about as if thrown down hastily and forgotten.

Ragged Cubans, black and white, swarmed everywhere. Naked children ran about dodging the flying feet of the horses that clattered along the cobblestones ridden by orderlies and officers. The houses, low one-storied buildings with heavily-barred and glassless windows, are painted in gaudy tones of blue, yellow and red. The rugged tile roofs, terra cotta in color, add to the picturesque look of these old, old houses. The effect on one is curious. The bottle-necked harbor filled with sunken ships, through which you creep to the city, has something to do with the feeling of utter dejection that seizes you. It is as if you were cut off from everything that is fresh, sweet and wholesome. You feel as if in some weird dream you have drifted into a city in fairyland, but a fairyland in which dwell disordered and dilapidated fairies. The place looks utterly hopeless.

The parting words of the kindly captain of the Vixen thrummed in your brain. "This is no place for a woman. If ever you needed a friend, you need one now. Stay close to Miss Barton and the Red Cross." No, it was no place for a woman—no place at all. Then came the thought of the brave creatures who were there wearing their lives out in the God-like work of nursing the ill. Clara Barton, no longer young, but as active, as clear of brain, as any woman of thirty-five. Far wiser than most, indeed. Clara Barton, working here day after day, in the heat, the stench; out at Siboney, close to the guns, feeding the hungry, nursing the wounded, with her little band of women, quiet, unassuming women—the very thought of it heartened one as one plodded down the white, dusty, baking street. Grumbling, indeed! Feeling hot and weary and dejected! The woman war correspondent was sadly in need of a good shaking.

Business is practically at a stand-still. The Cubans, fed by Miss Barton, seem to have fallen into a stolid and stupid lethargy. They hang around the doors of the Red Cross barn or trail about the streets, or sit in the marketplace cooking queer things on ill-smelling oil stoves. Greasy food, smelling of garlic, dark in color and repulsive to the stomach, lies simmering in saucepans and pots, and all about sit women, unwholesome-looking women, nearly all black, and only half-clothed.

Some of these women wear a single, cotton garment, a sort of long, untidy wrapper, which they trail after them in the dirt and dust. Others, with an attempt at coquetry, have pinned absurd colored gewgaws in their hair, and display, spread over their shoulders, shawls of pink and blue. Sometimes you will come upon a creature showing in her thin and withered throat and flattened bosom where Hunger had fastened her terrible claws. But amid all I found some of the laughter, some of the carelessness, some of the childishness, that you always find among the dark races who take life less seriously than we of the North do.

The morning sun blazed down—upon the body of a dead negro that lay there in the street. The upper part of this body, naked and withered, was emaciated, and one foot was swollen to a vast size. A few rags clothed his trunk. When I passed that way at noon the body was still where it had fallen. People went by uncaringly. I spoke with some, asking that the dead man be removed. But at four in the afternoon it still lay there. A dead man left to lie in the public street of a tropical city, under the blinding glare of a July sun! Small wonder that Yellow Jack—that horrible, ravaging Spanish pirate—is already beginning to creep upon the city of Santiago.

The grey mist lifted from the sea, and she awoke and stretched out her white arms, embracing the coast. The little waves began to leap and break. Child-waves these, that would grow to strong youth with the growing of the day, and would beat and clamour against the hills, seeking entrance. Through the beauty of this tropical morning, our little ship sped on. We were heading for Nima-Nima, that spot on the coast five and a half miles west of the port where, on July 3rd, the cruiser Infanta Maria Teresa was beached. We were bound for the whole run—about forty-eight miles from Santiago—that was taken by Admiral Cervera's fleet on the day when Spain's light as a naval power was quenched in the wild surf that leaps against the hills of Cuba. [The vaunted Spanish squadron of four cruisers and two destroyers had been smashed by the U.S. fleet in an epic battle beginning near Santiago Harbor and ending along the Cuban coastline. A similar naval triumph in Manila Bay helped the

United States win the eight-month-long war and gain possession of the Philippines, Guam, and Puerto Rico.]

The first ship to go under and head for beach was, as you know, the flagship Maria Teresa. She was still lying with her huge bows upon the beach, and her stern half under water. A great grey discolored hulk. A ghastly ship, with torn sides and battered decks. Half a mile further on, at Juan Gomalez, the Almirante Oquendo lay, half upon the beach, like some dying monster that had tried to crawl out of the sea, and died horribly in the attempt. We boarded the flagship, that is, we crept as best we could from beam to beam of the torn deck, and peered into what had been the cabin of the Spanish Admiral Cervera. We saw a charred and battered little room.

Further along the deck, a little heap of ashes, among which a few bones lingered, told its own story of horror. Nearby lay a sword and pistol. Awful was the ruin everywhere. Half-burnt rope ends dangled from the masts. Torn edges of iron flared outward. You would think an army of demons had been let loose from hell to twist and smash and batter the ships, to torture and burn and wreck impish cruelties on the men and beasts. What these Spanish soldiers must have suffered on that July day in the smoke and heat and stress of this terrible battle cannot be told by human lips, nor written by any pen. What the mental suffering was when despair seized them and death in his most awful shape boarded these ships can never be imagined.

For to see the ruin of them days after the worst had happened made the heart grow cold with the horror and misery of it all. Brave men and gallant fighters were these Spanish sailors. Men worn with hunger and sickness. Their flag has gone under, their great ships lie upon the shores of Cuba battered and twisted and done for, but they are monuments to the valor and desperation of the men of Spain, men who had not surrendered, who died fighting for the honor of the flag they loved. Poor Spain! The underdog in the fight, lying throttled there on the rocks by the bulldog hold of the great Anglo-Saxon. One could not offer her in the hour of her fall a tear of pity, but one could afford to shed for her the tear of sympathy.

The sun grew to his full heat as the day wore, and, leaving these melancholy wrecks, we sped on further out to where the

Vizcaya and the Colon were lying. The sea grew angry. The surf
leaped and foamed against the forefoot of the lonely hills who,
their heads in the clouds, did not hear its petulant clamouring.
Fifteen miles west, at Acerraderos, the Vizcaya lies in a half-
charred heap against the foothills. Was it not the Vizcaya that I
saw one little year ago curtseying on the waters of the Solent in
England to the battleship Brooklyn, who in turn bowed her compliments, while both ships did honor to the Queen's Jubilee?
Some such recollection drifted through one's mind at sight of the
poor broken thing that was lying here under the shadow of the
Cuban hills. She had blown up as she touched shore—a useless,
pitiful, old grey hulk.

The Colon had made a gallant race for life. Somehow one felt
towards her as towards a race-horse that, with breaking heart
and strained eyes, leaps towards the post in a mad effort to win
the race, but feeling his limbs failing and his sight dimming. She
is lying almost on the beach at Rio Tarquino, about forty-eight
miles from Santiago, on her beam ends, with seven of her guns
pointed at the sky and one of her propeller screws standing up
out of the water. The only one of the ships to haul down her flag
as she went to ruin upon the shore.

Sad sights, these ruined ships—speaking with no small voice
against the awful cruelty of war, the pitilessness of men when set
as foe one against the other—crying out there, dumb things as
they are, against man's inhumanity to man, against the breaking
of the great covenant of the Brotherhood of Man! And yet necessary say the gentlemen that from Senate houses and Parliaments
guide the destinies of nations. Perhaps, but a sad necessity, the
very saddest that the world will ever know.

The International Press Union of Women Journalists held their
rendezvous in the parlors of Willard's Hotel instead of the great
hall of the university because that learned institution had run
out of coal and couldn't get any for love or money. So you paid
four dollars to a cabby for crawling with you three blocks, and
tried to look as if your purse were not groaning. And you read
your little paper in fear and trembling before a solemn audience
of special correspondents and editors and you wished you were
any place on earth, even Santiago, Cuba, rather than standing

under that stream of light, reading something you didn't understand, in a strange voice you never heard before.

You had to steady yourself against the table or you would have fallen flat down, and your hands shivered so that the leaves of your paper began a tremolo symphony of their own that was fearsome. You gaped vacantly when the vigorous old lady in bob-tails asked you to tell her why Clara Barton didn't take you with the Red Cross people when Secretary Alger telegraphed her to do so, and you wondered where that nimble-minded old person got her knowledge. But you didn't reply to her. You were too far gone in fear. Instead, you told them all that there never was or could be a finer country anywhere than Canada or a grander paper than the *Mail and Empire*. But they never cheered. The aged person in bob-tails uttered a mild grunt and the two young male reporters attending smiled superciliously.

You rushed wildly on, and finished with a spurt that fairly winded you. There was no applause when you sat down. The chairman proposed a standing vote of thanks but people were busy talking and forgot to stand up until a smart rapping of the gavel recalled them. But there was no enthusiasm. All your fine allusions to "the boys in blue" fell flat, and even your reference to that noble battle hymn, The Star-Spangled Banner, failed to bring down the house. The next day the papers ignored you. They gave long recitations to the speech of the lady who spoke before you and the lady who spoke after you, but you were extinguished. The day after that, they remembered you! They gave your name and even the first line of your maiden speech, which was the dullest of the many dull ones, and so you were immortalized after all.

The world has been drenched in blood by land and sea. When will the command "Halt!" ring down the line? Unfortunate women of Russia who pay war's toll with their hearts. It was apprehended that the Czar might take his own life in the hour of overwhelming humiliation. He is not strong enough to do so, but he can cheerfully sacrifice the lives of his people. The case of Russia is so terrible, so filled with despair, that the hardest human heart, the dullest intellect, must feel pity. Yet some of the press comments have been almost brutal. The beast is large with

us, else why the excitement over a fight, the mad joy that surrounds the victor, the thumbs down for the vanquished? Why
war at all? The world ought to be sick of it. Humanity has surely
been staggered to the limit. Perhaps satiety will bring peace forever.

The Russ-Jap war is the greatest illustration the cause of temperance ever had. The Japanese silent, steadfast, clear of brain,
alert, muscular to an astonishing degree. The water-drinkers
against the Russians, enervated, timid, muddled with wine, slow
of movement, discouraged, dragging about with them enormous
stores of vodka and champagne, indulging in carousals while at
the very seat of war and defeated on every occasion. A more
powerfully illustrated argument in favor of temperance has
never been offered.

The hot afternoon sun shone on the autumn glory of the trees on
the avenue, and the still-green poplars on Elm Street, and everywhere there were crowds of people, and urchins on the branches
of trees, and babies in perambulators, and children squatting patiently on the edge of the sidewalk. From afar came the dull
thrumming of drums and the skirl of pipes and blast of bugle.
The people were massing about the Armouries, were pouring in
through the big doors, climbing to the galleries, crowding about
the soldiers of the Queen; all were gathered to speed that slender
band of comrades on the first march of the long journey that was
to lead them to where the great heart of Britain was pulsing its
highest and swiftest.

Women of all ranks, from the officers' wives who are treated to
puddings and pies, to those souls whose food in the battle of life
is always skilly, mixed freely together. If ever self and rank and
fashion and frivolity were forgotten it was the day we gathered,
men and women, one in heart and soul, to see our boys off to
fight for their Queen and Empire in South Africa. A soul-stirring
sight it was to see Toronto's four volunteer regiments massed in
the vast hall. The hall resounded with the hurrahs of the vast
throng, which had gathered together to do honor to the thin line
of heroes who are going to represent Canada in the fight for
right and liberty on a far continent, who were offering the best
that man has to offer—their lives.

The blood leaped riotously in one's veins after the bugle shrilled its call. The Grenadiers made a vivid patch of color as they massed in the centre while, beside them, steadfast, compact, stood by the great body of dark-clothed men who form Canada's finest regiment, the Queen's Own Rifles. But those on whom all eyes fixed with pride and affection were the men who carried the haversacks on their hips, our unit in the Canadian contingent. They looked fit, but there were signs on many a young face that showed how pride was struggling with grief, how love of country was battling with love of home and mother.

Behold the colonel—adored by the populace—good Colonel Otter, with his simple, dignified, manly and modest bearing. Ladies climb up the rickety ladder to the platform. Ladies weak of voice but strong in gifts. Things are showered on Colonel Otter. You could tell he would rather face a regiment of Boers with Kruger at their head than this array of field glasses, revolvers, cheques, and young ladies, but he bears up bravely. He salutes, and in a voice that vibrates with emotion, he tells the people how grateful he and his men are; how they will never forget this day; how they will give a good account of themselves if they get the chance.

Great as was the crowd at the drill-hall and on the streets, it appeared small compared with the mass of people that heaved and surged about the Union Station and alongside the troop-train. When the boys came into the station after their long march from the Armouries, it was a straight fight for footing all the way down the platform and we were in the thick of it.

Young soldiers leaned from train windows and kissed the girls who climbed up the side to say good-bye. The boys wore roses on their breasts and in their caps, last love-gifts from tender hands. Shouting, rejoicing, grieving and struggling, people strove passionately to grasp once more the hands outstretched from the windows and cry, "God bless you, boys!" One man called to a big policeman to bring his mother to him, and the strong arm of the law flashed out and guided the woman to her son's side. There was no active grief apparent in her face. She seemed to be sunk in a stupor, without much sense or feeling left but that he was going from her and might never come back.

A big sergeant was crying like a girl because he was not going.

Girls waved flags as they swayed hither and thither, caught in the crowd like reeds in a storm. Pushing, jostling, now onward, now back, we fought our way. Once hands were stretched out—whose hands I will never know—with a quiet, "Good-bye, Kit." Then the crowd surged again, and the wave carried us down the line as the train groped its way cautiously out. I had seen the going away of the army to Cuba, and had been stirred by it, but never stirred as one was when the Canadian contingent passed away to face their fate and make history for their country.

18. WORDS OF WISDOM

By today's standards, Kit's writing was often overly dramatic, her theories too simplistic, her phraseology a trifle awkward. But she never bored her readers. Indeed, she believed that while integrity and accuracy were essential, a columnist also had to be outrageously opinionated and never, ever, become a dull, mild-mannered hack. In this respect, she was an entertainer, putting on a show in the same way the comedians and jugglers did at local vaudeville houses. She was willing to admit that the vaudeville artists actually influenced her technique. "A writer can learn an important lesson by listening to the best comics," she said in an 1897 speech at the Toronto Public Library. "They do not waste sentences. They say a great deal in a short period of time." Starky White was Kit's favorite comedian. A Boston monologuist, he played Shea's theater in Toronto on a semi-regular basis, centering his routine on the perils of heavy drinking, a subject of which he apparently had unlimited personal knowledge. Starky was exceptionally adept at audience exchanges: he would answer questions from spectators with sharply honed, one-line rejoinders that brought down the house. His appeal for Kit was understandable, as she too was a master of neatly worded one-liners. Her pithy comments on life—what you might term bits of hearth-side philosophy—were so effective that a New York publisher made an unsuccessful try to have her write an entire book of pungent sayings. Some of Kit's remarks, especially the aphorisms, were as witty as those produced by another celebrated turn-of-the-century scribe, Bob Edwards of the Calgary Eye Opener.

If you want a successful marriage, always have time for your husband—but never too much.

It is curious that men, even the most intelligent and travelled men, cannot be got to understand how child-like women are in many ways.

We women have our faults but we are generally generous to the male sex. Did we not offer them a bite of the apple?

Pathos expressed by restraint, instead of gush, is the more powerful.

Laziness is a vice so generally possessed by women that they do not tolerate it, let alone appreciate it, in the other sex. Not to have to get up too early is the average woman's idea of bliss so long as the poor early bird has been pushed off to his business to catch his worm. Men must work and women must sleep is their motto.

Try to remember that you can never love any individual entirely until you laugh at him a little.

The savageness of female cruelty has a certain fascination about it—to a survivor.

There is no more charming girl in all the world than she who is attentive to old ladies.

It is a curious fact that more widows than widowers marry again. Perhaps we find the men more agreeable in the matrimonial harness than they find us.

All sorts of stupid people are being pitch-forked into the already choked-up professionals, such as law, owing to the railroading system of education in Canada.

Candor is a virtue for which women pay most dearly.

When clever boys attempt to be witty, they usually make fools of themselves.

Habit is not happiness but it is an apology for it with which many long-married couples have to be content.

The happiness of a marriage rests not on passion but on affection. Passion will not heed argument, but affection listens and lasts.

When a woman has made up her mind to love a hero, and only a hero, the man who loves that woman will do well to conceal a live mouse in his clothes the next time he visits her and to let the tiny beast escape at the psychological moment.

Nothing kills love, not coldness, not indifference, not even harshness of speech and manner, as contempt and revulsion. Contempt and revulsion born to the woman who has been struck by the hand of the man she once loved.

It is no use attempting to converse with cranks. As soon as you discover their crankism, fly. The same as you would from a leper, a thug, or a Boxer. Don't vacillate. The path of duty when you recognize the crank, whether he is the psychic, the religious, the artistic, the vegetarian crank, or whatever, is to flee. Cross the street. Wait in a shop till he has gone by. If he is going by the same train take the next, or buy a ticket for one going in the opposite direction. Your time is too precious to be wasted talking to anyone who is out of his mind on any one subject.

Few women are so ugly as to cancel out that enchanting charm which the right of our sex gives to all women.

Those self-effacing, meek, ultra-conscientious wives are the ones that spoil the husbands. They become a bore, like the aggressively neat women from which the Lord preserves us.

The man who asks a woman to give up everything—reputation, duty, for him—and who proves worthy of the sacrifice—is yet to be born.

Old maids are the wise virgins of this earth. The married women took the terrible men they refused.

Society men are unfair to girls. Directly two people are introduced, the man begins to make conversation to suit the lower (?) intelligence of his companion. Women often follow this lead because they think he doesn't know much and therefore can only indulge in inane remarks. What can a bright girl think of a man who chatters about tennis and the weather, or hails compliments as big as hen's eggs at her? No doubt the man tries his hardest to make small talk. If he would only try a size or two larger, he would be agreeably surprised at his success.

One yearns for the toy called fame, and cries at intervals for it all his life long. If he gets it, he finds a bladder that shrivels with the first pin-prick.

Was there ever a friendship between two women that did not mean a plot against a third?

While a man loves a beautiful woman, he will absolutely adore an ugly one—once he loves her.

Was there ever a daughter of Eve who did not play havoc with a man's Paradise—or else make it?

As for scandal, the human mind must have something to grind. It is as insatiable as the human stomach.

Men have so much in their power. They can save so many women.

Ideals, hope, ambitions tumble into ruins before the necessity of gaining daily bread.

There is not a heart that ever beat that did not know its own breaking.

Woman is woman's most implacable enemy.

It is a fine thing to be a trifle vain. Too much modesty does not pay in this world.

On the dunghills of life, we sometimes find the sweetest flowers growing.

If you run after popularity, you will never catch it.

A subject that is perfectly beautiful does not appeal to the true artist. It lacks imperfection.

The most successful men with women are those who do the least. The man who keeps a girl expecting that he is going to kiss her, and never does, is the one that—well, the one that she would really let kiss her. If a man kisses a girl outright, she would either be offended or she would have to pretend that she was. The wise man lets his lips brush her hair or rest on the handle of her fan near her fingertips, or if he is very bold, he lightly kisses her eyes instead of her rosy mouth.

Half of our human wreckage come from the dry-root of disuse.

The man who loves to change the object of his highest feelings is one who is hardly capable of high feelings in the true sense.

The world holds a larger share of sorrow than joy, and it ought to be a consolation to know that we will not live forever. To be robbed of death would be the most frightful thing that could happen to us.

To the man you love, tell all. To other men, tell nothing.

Women are the shorn lambs of Fate.

Revolutions are created not by the strength of an idea but the intensity of an emotion.

Friendship is far more tragic than love. It lasts longer.

Civilization is assuredly the state of things which generates ennui and supplies the readiest means of dissipating it.

Cynicism is the worst ailment of the soul from which man or woman can suffer.

The arrogance of youth would be unbearable if it were not so amusing.

If a lady treads on a banana skin and sprinkles herself all over the sidewalk, a man will gallantly gather up the pieces and help her to place herself together again. But if his own wife meets with a similar misfortune, he gives her a piece of his mind, if he happens to have any, and makes things hot for a week or so. To those we love we are grizzly bears, and to those we don't we are as polite as dancing masters. It is a queer world.

The most noticeable thing about summer resorts is the paucity of men. Where do the men go, or are they dying off, leaving the world to the women and thus proving the survival of the fittest?

There is no form of human agony so bitter as that caused by a loveless marriage.

That proverb about absence making the heart grow fonder applies more to patriotic feelings than the love for each other.

The girl a man would marry at twenty, he would not dream of marrying when he is thirty.

A gentleman cannot win a girl by kissing her while she is fast asleep. The only thing he will win is her profound contempt.

It is a sad house where the hen crows louder than the cock.

Woman can be bourgeoise in her attitude towards man. She wants him to be telling her she is charming, or praising something about her, if only her gown. When he gives her the highest gift—his mind, his soul, the best of him—she says that he is dull.

Youth is almost a necessity in matters of love for it can discount beauty. Small wonder, then, that women cling to it and ape its appearance long after it has left them.

Men have very direct and uncomplicated minds, yet they are the most blundering, clumsy creatures imaginable.

A sure way to escape old age and its consequent disabilities is to work yourself so hard that you will die young.

Some pessimists believe that whenever they see two people happy it means the misery of a third.

If a man consults his powers of reasoning, and only those powers, he would never marry.

One reason why men are so ready to deny a woman a sense of humor is because the object of our humor is pretty apt to be a man.

A bit of humor is a necessity in the make-up of the modern woman. It is an ingredient that ensures sanity.

There is little use in loud-voiced condemnation of things we do not understand. The bray of the ass drowns all other sounds but that of his own voice.

Imitation may be the sincerest form of flattery but it is certainly not the best form of style. Any writer with a claim to individuality creates a style of his own.

Women are learning to talk and the woman who can talk best is the most thoroughly popular. There are countless ways of talking and a display of learning is not a requisite. Some of the most brilliant people are hopeless bores at the dinner table. The art of conversation is to be bright, quick, turning easily in any given direction, and adept at listening—for half of conversation should be listening—and to be witty, without being vulgar, and, occasionally, epigrammatic. It is supposed too often that stupid, dense men dislike a woman the reverse of themselves but this is solely when she is sarcastic and repels others instead of drawing them out. The dull man usually admires the good-natured, clever woman who shows off her mental paces for his delectations.

The most acute cases of marital suffering are not the degradation, curses and blows that are the outcome of sheer brutality. They come from quietly unhappy couples who both love and hate each other.

It is a tremendous shame that women should be lectured on their bad manners—and an even more tremendous shame that we need it.

A man's ideal is not wounded when a woman fails in worldly wisdom; but if in grace, in tact, in propriety, in kindness, in delicacy, she should be found wanting, his heart receives an inward hurt.

It is a much harder job to keep a man's love than to win it. It will not be done by pretty dresses and pretty looks. These are, in a way, essential; at least, the neat gowns are, but the dress was never beautiful enough, nor the face of the woman who wears it fair enough, to reconcile a man to burnt potatoes, soggy bread and leathery steak. For a man is practical in his love-making, and how much more so when his beloved is his own, all doubts and fears having been settled at the altar. A man wants a dainty wife, but his creature comforts must not be sacrificed to this daintiness. Neither need the thorough, efficient housewife hope for justice if her praiseworthy efforts are made in gowns that are frights and if her hair is always in curl-papers.

Pay not the slightest attention to the malice of lying tongues. There will always be screeching jays in the woods.

Nothing in the world is worth striving for—not riches, not fame, not power—more than domestic peace.

You needn't be proud of yourself because Nature makes you love somebody. Nature, after all, does the same service for monkeys.

"Please give us a minute definition of what you call a gentleman," asks a correspondent. Well, in my opinion, a gentleman ceases to be one when he has to be defined.

A plain-faced woman who makes the man whom she loves believe she knows not the meaning of worry, and who constantly has for him a pleasant smile, and a word of welcome, will discover that tender thoughts of her are creeping down further into his heart than those of the beautiful girl whom she envies.

Women rarely allow their real nature to appear. Self-suppression has been drilled into them during the ages until it has become a habit. Many a wild dream, a daring project, a tumultuous passion, lies hidden behind the calm barrier of a woman's heart. Underneath her calm, commonplace exterior, there is often a fierce, clamorous nature, clamorous for joy, for action, for independence. I ask every girl who is bending over her typewriter in a businessman's office, who is pounding the machine in the sweat shop, who is eternally washing dishes and scrubbing floors as a domestic servant, who is going out night after night in society to dance or dinner, if I am not right. There is not a woman living who has not had her secret dreams—never to be realized!—but not the less real for all that. And there is not one man in a thousand who has ever seen into the depths of a woman's heart.

"Kit"

Gentle lady of our love,
Fast asleep you live;
'Tis the parting of the ways;
Comrade of so many days,
We must say good-bye.

You were made of rose and pearl,
Fire and snow and dew;
And a Spirit naught could tame
Burned as free as wind-blown flame,
In the heart of you.

All the lowly—all the blind—
All the lost and lone;
These you stooped to, with a smile;
These you found, and loved awhile;
These you made your own.

From the earth so dark with woe,
From the troubled sea,
Toward the lovely land of light
Thy sweet soul doth take its flight,
In good company.

Yet me thinks that even now,
On your outward way,
You will pass o'er fields of pain,
And will comfort once again
Those by whom you stay!

Virna Sheard, Toronto Globe, 1915

CHRONOLOGY

1864   Born Kathleen Blake, near Galway in western Ireland, into a socially prominent family.

1880   Marries George Willis, a wealthy country squire forty years her senior.

1884–89   Widowed at age twenty, she emigrates to Toronto, Canada, where she supports herself doing secretarial work. Later marries her boss, Edward Watkins, and moves with him to Winnipeg, where she has two children. Thady and Pat.

1889   Returns to Toronto after her husband's sudden death and is hired by the *Toronto Mail* as Canada's first women's page editor. Launches a weekly column that includes the country's first lovelorn advice section.

1893   Covers the World Columbian Exposition in Chicago.

1897   Goes to England to cover Queen Victoria's Diamond Jubilee celebration where she is Prime Minister Sir Wilfrid Laurier's guest at a Buckingham Palace medal-giving ceremony.

1898   Marries Dr. Theobald Coleman. Interviews Sarah Bernhardt backstage at a Montreal theater. Spends a month in Cuba observing and commenting upon the Spanish American War, thus becoming history's first accredited woman war correspondent.

1899   Moves with her husband, Dr. Coleman, to Copper
         Cliff, Ontario, a northern mining community. .

1901   Moves with her husband to Hamilton, Ontario.

1904   Helps found the Canadian Women's Press Club and is
         appointed its first president.

1905   Gains an exclusive interview with the notorious fraud
         artist Cassie Chadwick in a Cleveland jail.

1906   Tours a seamy underground community after the
         earthquake and fire that devastated San Francisco.

1907   Covers the Harry K. Thaw murder trial in New York.

1911   Leaves the *Toronto Mail and Empire* to become Can-
         ada's first syndicated columnist.

1915   Dies in Hamilton, Ontario, aged fifty-one.

SOURCES

The excerpts from "Woman's Kingdom" were obtained by going through the *Toronto Mail* and the *Mail and Empire* files at the Metropolitan Toronto Central Library, the Archives of Ontario in Toronto, Concordia University in Montreal, Carleton University in Ottawa, the University of British Columbia in Vancouver, and the University of Alberta in Edmonton. I also acquired biographical material from the *Toronto Globe and Mail*, the *Toronto Star*, the now-defunct *Toronto Telegram*, the Hamilton branch of the Media Club of Canada, the *Hamilton Spectator*, and the Edmonton Public Library. Special thanks must go to K. R. Macpherson, Tina James, Bonnie Buxton, L. R. Lupack, Mabel Burkholder, Anne Mack, Donald Watt, and Helen Johnston.

Three articles that provided insights into Kit Coleman's character were "Kit, the Journalist," by Emily Weaver, *Canadian Magazine*, August 1917; "Queen of the Sob Sisters," by David MacDonald, *Maclean's*, January 1953, and "The Vagaries of a Woman's Page," by Kit Coleman, *Winnipeg Free Press*, June 9, 1906. Books that were helpful to my research included *Leading Ladies: Canada 1639–1967*, by Jean Bannerman (Highland Press, Galt, Ontario, 1967); *The First Casualty*, by Phillip Knightly (Harcourt Brace Jovanovich, New York, 1975); *News and the Southams*, by Charles Bruce (Macmillan, Toronto, 1968); *Toronto*, by Bruce West (Doubleday Canada Ltd., Toronto, 1967); *Gay Canadian Rogues*, by Frank Rasky (Thomas Nelson and Sons, Toronto, 1957); *The Correspondents' War*, by Charles H. Brown (Charles Scribner's Sons, New York, 1967); *The Kingdom of Canada*, by W. L. Morton (Bobbs-Merrill, New York, 1963); *Cycling*, by W. A. Robertson (F. Pratt and Co., Stratford, Ontario, 1894); *The Canadian Style*, edited by Raymond Reid (Fitzhenry and Whiteside, Toronto, 1973); *Toronto: The Romance of a Great City,* by Katherine Hale (Cassel and Co. Ltd., Toronto, 1956), and *Never Done,* (Canadian Women's Educational Press, Toronto, 1976).